AMERICANS IN ENGLAND

HENRY ADAMS

AMERICANS

IN ENGLAND

ROBERT B. MOWAT

With Illustrations

Essay Index Reprint Series

BOOKS FOR LIBRARIES PRESS
FREEPORT, NEW YORK

STANDARD BOOK NUMBER:
8369-1423-6

LIBRARY OF CONGRESS CATALOG CARD NUMBER:
79-99642

PRINTED IN THE UNITED STATES OF AMERICA

PREFACE

THE idea of writing this account of the Americans who for longer or shorter periods have sojourned in England came to me as the result of delightful and fruitful months and years spent at various times in the United States. Englishmen have often told of their experiences in America. What have Americans thought of their life in England? This was the question which occurred to me as I was packing my trunk for the *Aquitania*, and thinking of the friends that I would meet again, the places I would see, the conversations I would renew, and the life I would take up once more, on this next visit to the United States.

On landing at New York in that springtime of 1930, I made a leisurely journey, by way of New Haven and Yale University, to Boston and Harvard. At Boston I called at Park Street at the historic office of Houghton Mifflin Company and had a talk with Mr. Ferris Greenslet, whom I had known in his literary haunts in London. Mr. Greenslet showed me his office library, indicated useful sources, and expressed approval of my notion of a book on *Americans in England*. So, after indulging a little longer in the literary and academic life of Boston and Cambridge, I went on my way to Cleveland, Ohio. There I spent the summer, in the lecture-room, library, and club of Western Reserve University, and in boulevards, parks, political meetings, and homes of that vigorous and enterprising city.

Americans in England is the result of studies made in
the libraries of Cleveland, Ohio; in conversations with
many academic friends in that state and in other states
of the Union; in many hours of pleasant work in the
libraries of Oxford, London, and my own home. It has
kept me, as it were, in cultured and warm-hearted
American society throughout the great depression of
1931–32, when Anglo-American social visits were by in-
exorable facts suspended.

A study of the life of Americans in England points
to the conclusions: that the Americans know England
before they come to it; that they are the best describers
of English society and of English country, as they see
it; and that as they have received much from English
life and art and letters, so have they given. This is so,
because, notwithstanding interesting and often striking
local differences and developments, the two people have
their civilisation and culture in common.

R. B. MOWAT

CONTENTS

ILLUSTRATIONS

AMERICANS IN ENGLAND

I

THEY COME AND GO

Visits of Englishmen to America have been frequent if not exactly common occurrences throughout the last hundred and fifty years; and for about three hundred and forty or three hundred and fifty years before then, from the time when Cabot and his crew sailed from Bristol (1497), visits from England were at any rate occasional. For a long time the visitors were only explorers and traders; exploring and trading were nearly always combined in the same persons. In the later part of the reign of Queen Elizabeth, after 1570, the voyages outward, from England, were made by people, many of whom had the purpose of settling overseas; for by the year 1570, England was supposed to be overcrowded; certain economic developments had dislocated industrial life, and a good many people were ready to quit their country. They were not, of course, visitors; they were immigrants or migrants. Genuine visitors, who went to see their kinsfolk and friends, or merely to satisfy the eternal curiosity of man's nature (the curiosity which alone keeps him spiritually alive), were few in number before the later eighteenth century; after that they increase and continue.

The impressions of British visitors to America, their appreciations of American life, have been selected and collected in an admirable literary conspectus.[1] The back-flow of visitors from America to Great Britain has, on the other hand, to a large extent escaped the notice of historians. Individually, the visits attracted notice, and left their mark on society and literature. Collectively, however, as a phase of Anglo-American life, they have not been given their due.

Their influence on Anglo-American affairs has been strong and beneficent. It is always good that there should be a frequent coming and going between peoples. If the stream both ways is steady and strong, friendship and mutual understanding must result. The English are great travellers; they have visited America in large numbers, and have made almost a habit of doing so since the end of the eighteenth century. They were not always appreciative; they were not even always discriminating; in the early nineteenth century their observations and their writings were, in many cases, greatly resented in America. The Englishmen gave themselves airs, and affected, or still worse felt, superiority. Washington Irving, writing about the year 1818,

[1] Allan Nevins, *American Social History as Recorded by British Travellers* (1924).

comments on this fact, 'observing the comparative importance and swelling magnitude of many English travellers among us, who, I am assured, were very little people in their own country.' [1] Since the middle of the nineteenth century, or, say, since the visit of Anthony Trollope during the Civil War or of Edward Prince of Wales shortly before, there has been no grievance, no ground for resentment, on the part of the Americans, regarding the attitude of the English when they visited the United States. There was, however, some such resentment in the early stages of Anglo-American relations, and there were reasons for it.

The English, on their side, never had reason to complain of the attitude of their American visitors. The Americans found in England the thing that they had dreamed of. They had grown up with a picture of England ever in their minds: the England of Hengist and Horsa, of Alfred the Great; of Harold, William the Norman, and the Plantagenets; Queen Elizabeth and Shakespeare; Johnson, Sir Walter Scott, and Thackeray. The native-born American, at any rate down to the middle of the nineteenth century, had always an England of his dreams.

> Her fame is constantly before him. He hears of her statesmen, her orators, her scholars, her philosophers, her divines, her patriots. In the nursery, he learns her ballads. Her poets train his imagination. Her language is his with its whole intellectual riches, past and for ever newly flowing; a tie, to use Burke's figure, light as air, and unseen; but stronger than links of iron.[2]

[1] Washington Irving, *Sketch-Book* (London, 1864), 3-4.
[2] Richard Rush, *A Residence at the Court of London* (1833), 11-12.

With beautiful thoughts like these flitting through his mind, the cultured American coming to England was 'sympathetic' to the country, was perhaps, after all, the true interpreter of it, for the England of our dreams is the real England, immutable beneath the spoiling hand of man.

The first famous American visitor, however, was not the cultured son or daughter of the early settlers of Virginia or Massachusetts, but a dusky woman of the ancient American race. Pocahontas,[1] the daughter of Powhatan, chief of an Indian tribe near Jamestown in Virginia, may or may not have saved Captain John Smith from death, when he was taken prisoner by the Indians in 1608. She was apparently only twelve years old then. It is certainly true that she herself was taken prisoner by the Jamestown settlers and held as a ransom, to pay for the freedom of some Englishmen who had fallen into Powhatan's hands. The prisoners, or most of them, were restored, but Pocahontas did not go back to her own people. She was baptised a Christian, and was married in 1613 to John Rolfe, a widower, 'one of the principal settlers,' who discovered how to cure tobacco for the English market. The marriage had the approval of the bride's father, Powhatan, and ensured during his life peace between the Jamestown settlers and the Indians. In 1616, Rolfe,

[1] There were two earlier Indians, Manteo and Wanchese, brought to England by the expedition of 1584 which Sir Walter Raleigh sent out to 'Virginia.' Both were baptised. Manteo returned to Virginia. Wanchese died in England in 1585 and is buried in Bideford: Doyle, *The English in America* (1882), 77, 95.

taking the first consignment of his cured tobacco-leaf with him, accompanied by Pocahontas and several other Indians, went to England along with Governor Dale who then left the Virginian settlement for good and all. Pocahontas, dressed like a fine lady of the reign of Elizabeth or James I, was presented at court by Lady Delaware, and naturally attracted attention; but nothing is known concerning what she thought of England, for she died at Gravesend, when on the point of sailing for Virginia, in March, 1617, probably of consumption, leaving a son, Thomas Rolfe, to carry on her race.[1] Her Indian companions mostly fared no better than herself. No more attempts were made to bring Indians to England.

Visitors from America to England were not common in the seventeenth century. The conditions of the voyage acted as a deterrent; it was expensive, dangerous, uncomfortable, and required six weeks or more on the sea. Few or none of the settlers of the northern or the southern colonies had the necessary means or the leisure for the voyage; all their time and energy were taken up in making their livelihood where they were. During the English Civil War, the northern colonists, the Puritans of New England, sympathised with the Parliamentarians or Roundheads; the men of the south, who were mainly Anglican in religion, stood for the king; but during the times of the Civil War and Commonwealth, the American colonies were practically independent. None of the native-born, so far as is

[1] D. Garnett, *Pocahontas* (1933), and Kathleen P. Woods, *The True Story of Captain John Smith* (1907), 349 ff.

known, came to England to take part in the struggle; except in Virginia there can scarcely have been any native-born Americans of military age when the Civil War began in 1642. The famous Sir George Downing, who gave his name to Downing Street, Whitehall, may perhaps be reckoned as an American in seventeenth-century England.

George Downing was the son of a London barrister and was born at Dublin (where his father, Emmanuel Downing, was probably in the Administration) in 1623. His mother, Lucy Winthrop, was the sister of John Winthrop, Governor of Massachusetts after 1629. Emmanuel Downing, who had removed from Dublin and was living with his wife and son in London, proposed to follow his brother-in-law to the New World. His wife was afraid that education in the colony would not be good enough for their son, and she actually suggested to John Winthrop, by letter, that a college should be started. As a matter of fact, when this suggestion was being made, and independently of it, the colony of Massachusetts was founding Harvard College. Two years later, in 1638, the Downings set forth and sailed, ultimately settling at Salem.

The young George Downing became an undergraduate at Harvard, and was one of the college's earliest students. He graduated at the first Commencement, held in 1642. Next year he was appointed an instructor, and held this position until 1645 when he became a ship's chaplain in the West Indies; from there he went to England and was a military chaplain, on the Parliamentary side, in the Civil War. When the Civil War was over, he might have been expected to return to Massachusetts, to his family and friends and to a career either in a church or in the Assembly. Nevertheless, the rest of Downing's life was spent in English politics and diplomacy. He was one of the active group of Independents who wanted to make Cromwell king. He undertook a successful mission to France (1655) in favour of the Vaudois who were being persecuted for their religion by France's ally, the Duke of Savoy. After this, he became ambassador for the Commonwealth at The Hague. In 1660 he entered into the service of Charles II, and was made Teller in the Exchequer, later Secretary of the Treasury, and had a distinguished career as an official. Tutor, chaplain, soldier, diplomatist, civil servant, member of Parliament, Sir George Downing, as he became, was an eminent, if not very lovable, public man. He had the reputation, Pepys says, of being terribly mean, but he was certainly a good and careful Treasury official. In 1681 he bought a 'messuage' in Whitehall, and built four houses, one of which, 'Number 10, Downing Street,' combined with a house behind, became in 1735 the official residence of Walpole and of all subsequent First Lords of the Treasury — that is, the Prime Ministers of Great Britain. Downing died in 1684 at his house in Cambridgeshire. His father and mother had returned in later life from Massachusetts, and George Downing himself never revisited the colony.

During the first thirty or forty years of the history of New England, there was a surprising amount of travelling between America and England. Henry Vane, aged twenty-two, the son of a Secretary of State of Charles I, came out to Massachusetts, along with John Winthrop the younger and Hugh Peters, in 1635. He was a man of high character and the best education. He was trained at Westminster School and Magdalen Hall, Oxford, and had served on a diplomatic mission to the Court of Austria. John Winthrop describes his arrival:

> Here cáme one Mr. Harry Vane, son and heir to Sir Henry Vane, controller of the King's house, who being a young gentleman of excellent parts, and had been employed by his father (when he was ambassador) in foreign affairs; yet being called to the obedience of the gospel, forsook the honours and preferments of the court, to enjoy the ordinances of Christ in their purity here.[1]

He had license from Charles I to stay three years. The freemen of the colony elected Vane Governor. He was young and inexperienced, so the great John Winthrop was made Deputy-Governor. Vane, however, disagreed with some regulations concerning immigration, passed by the General Court, so he left Massachusetts in 1637 and never came back. Later, he was famous as one of the leaders of the Parliament against Charles I, and although not one of the 'Regicides' who tried the king and had him executed, was condemned for treason after the Restoration and executed on Tower Hill, London, in 1662.

Edward Winslow was a genuine American, if being a founder makes him such. He was one of the Leyden congregation which went to make up the band of Pilgrim Fathers of 1620. After the founding of the

[1] Winthrop, *History of New England* (ed. 1853), I, 203.

colony of Massachusetts, he took a leading part in its administration, holding the positions of Assistant-Governor and Governor for twenty years. He found time to revisit England four times — in 1623, 1624, 1635, and 1646, on each occasion representing the colonists in negotiations with the Crown. It is clear that the political atmosphere of England during the 'Personal Government' of Charles I was uncongenial to the New England Puritans; Winslow, on his third visit (1635), found the hand of Archbishop Laud heavy. John Winthrop wrote:

> Mr. Winslow, the late governour of Plimouth, being this year in England, petitioned the council there for a commission to withstand the intrusions of the French, and Dutch... but the archbishops, being incensed against him, as against all these plantations, informed the rest, that he was a separatist etc., and that he did not marry etc., and thereupon gate him committed; but after some months, he petitioned the board, and was discharged.[1]

On his last visit, 1646 and the following years, Winslow became deeply involved, not merely in the affairs of New England, but in the religious controversies of Old England as well. In 1650 the 'courtly pilgrim' entered the service of the Commonwealth as a member of the 'Committee for Compounding with Delinquents.' In 1655 he went out as a Civil Commissioner in the fleet which Cromwell despatched against the Spanish West Indies. After the capture of Jamaica by the fleet, Winslow died of fever, May 8, 1655. He had left his wife and children in Massachusetts when he sailed to England in 1646 and never saw them again.

[1] Winthrop, *History of New England*, I, 205.

The Puritan Fathers had declared that they remained
part of the Church of England, but in practice they
carried on their worship and regulated the congrega-
tions in Massachusetts after the manner of the English
Independents. A certain Dr. Child (a Doctor of Medi-
cine of Padua) made trouble in 1646, by agitating for
the use of Presbyterian ways. He was severely repri-
manded by the magistrates, and was put in prison.
Being soon released, however, he went to England,
where, apparently, a supporter, Mr. Thomas Fowle,
had preceded him. The interests and good name of
Massachusetts were ably defended by Edward Winslow,
as agent for the colony. There were other men of
Massachusetts in England who stood up for their
people. Dr. Child was evidently a rather passionate
man. The first historian of New England describes
the upshot of this affair in his casual and quaint manner.
The incident occurred in 1648.

> Dr. Child preferred a petition to the committee against
> us, and put in Mr. Thomas Fowle his name among others;
> but he, hearing of it, protested against it, (for God had
> brought him very low both in his estate and in his reputa-
> tion since he joined in the first petition). After this, the
> Doctor, meeting with Mr. Willoughby upon the Exchange
> (this Mr. Willoughby dwelt at Charlestown, but his father
> was a colonel of the city), and falling in talk about New
> England, the Doctor railed against the people, saying
> they were a company of rogues and knaves; Mr. Wil-
> loughby answered that he who spoke so, etc., was a knave,
> whereupon the Doctor gave him a box on the ear. Mr.
> Willoughby was ready to have closed with him, etc., but
> being upon the exchange, he was stayed, but presently
> arrested him. And when the Doctor saw the danger he

was in, he employed some friends to make his peace, who ordered him to give five pounds to the poor of New England (for Mr. Willoughby would have nothing of him), and to give Mr. Willoughby open satisfaction in the full exchange, and to give it under his hand, never to speak evil of New England men after, nor to occasion any trouble to the country, or to any of the people, all which he gladly performed; and besides God had so blasted his estate, as he was quite broken, etc.[1]

London in the Civil War and under the Commonwealth was a magnet for the stern Congregationalists and Independents of New England. 'Then, for some years, the ships carried more passengers eastward than they brought westward.'[2] It was characteristic of those times that ministers of religion were also men of affairs, engaged in politics, in army administration, in diplomacy, even in the law, though few became quite so eminent in civil administration as Sir George Downing. One of the most soul-stirring, one of the most influential, New Englanders in London under Oliver Cromwell was Hugh Peters. He was a Cornishman, an M.A. of Trinity College, Cambridge, an ordained minister of the Church of England. As a Puritan clergyman, however, he found life in the Church under Laud uncongenial. He moved to Holland, and in 1632 was pastor of the English congregation at Rotterdam. In 1635 he went out to New England where he had many friends, among others his relation by marriage, John Winthrop.

[1] Winthrop, *History of New England*, II, 391–92.
[2] Channing, *History of the United States*, I, 332.

Hugh Peters was always brimful of an energy which expressed itself in manifold directions. He was an earnest, vivid, and moving preacher; he was active in church administration; he was a keen and helpful critic of social policy, poor-law, and such matters; he engaged, zealously, almost furiously, in theological controversy. In Massachusetts he speedily acquired strong influence, and was one of the chief prosecutors in the trial of Mrs. Anne Hutchinson, the religious enthusiast and mystic who was condemned and banished by the General Court of Massachusetts in 1637. In the following lean and difficult years in the colony, Peters was one of the most resourceful leaders, inaugurating measures for the increase of trade and for the relief of distress which won him a unique position in public confidence. In 1641 the colony sent him to London as agent, to negotiate for further support from the friends of Massachusetts in England, for times were hard in New England, and emigration from the old country and investment had almost stopped. Peters brought his wife to England, but she returned to the colony in 1645 and he never saw her again. He represented the colony ably and successfully in London, but when the Civil War broke out he was caught up into the maelstrom of politics and militarism, became a chaplain to the Parliamentary forces, and envoy to Holland, a preacher to hesitating recruits, a kind of Grand Inquisitor at once severe and compassionate, attending political prisoners to the scaffold and administering encouragement and comfort in their last moments. His influence as a preacher and speaker on

the Parliamentary side was unexampled; Fairfax and
Cromwell habitually employed him, whether it was to
exhort the forlorn hope beneath the walls of a belea-
guered town, or to persuade the reluctant Parliament
to engage more decisively and expensively in the
war.

Peters now seemed to the New England friends who
visited him one of the happiest of men, or at any rate
a man who ought to have been one of the happiest.
He had a pension of £200 a year granted by Parliament,
and paid out of a forfeited Royalist estate; he had rooms
assigned him in Whitehall Palace; he had a scholar's
library, that of the executed Archbishop Laud, conferred
upon him by Parliament; he was in the centre of affairs,
busy, respected, powerfully influential, contributing to
the public weal. Yet Roger Williams of Rhode Island,
visiting him in 1654 at Whitehall, found the great
man with a secret cause of anxiety and disquiet—
the state of his wife's mind and the drain upon his
resources. 'He himself told me,' wrote Williams to
John Winthrop, 'that that library wherein we were
was Canterbury's and given him by the Parliament.
His wife lives from him, not wholly, but much, distracted. He tells me he has but £200 a year, and he
allowed her four score *per annum* of it. Surely the most
holy Lord is most wise in all the trials He exerciseth
his people with. He told me that his affliction for his
wife stirred him up to action abroad, and when success
tempted him to pride, the bitterness in his bosom-
comforts was a cooler and a bridle to him.'[1]

[1] Masson, *Life of Milton* (1877), IV, 533.

All this activity was to lead him far, though never back to Massachusetts. After the Restoration, Peters was seized and accused, falsely, of having been one of those who compassed directly the life of the king, Charles I. On October 16, 1660, he was executed at Charing Cross, maintaining his spirit with the same fortitude and equanimity, the same sure hope of a glorious resurrection, to which he had so fervently exhorted Royalists when a similar fate was upon them.

Roger Williams, to whom Hugh Peters had confided his secret trouble, was a native of London, ordained a minister of the Church of England, and had gone out to Massachusetts in the *Lyon*, in 1631. He was more averse from the ways of the English Church even than the Massachusetts 'Independents'; he was a Separatist. Being expelled from the colony in 1635, he went off with some faithful followers and founded the colony of Rhode Island. In 1643 he went to England on the business of his colony, was successful in obtaining from the Commissioners of the Long Parliament a charter of incorporation, and made John Milton's acquaintance.[1]   As a place of religious liberty, Rhode Island attracted settlers and flourished. In 1651 he paid a second, long visit to England on the affairs of the colony, and renewed his friendship with Milton. This was in every way congenial to Williams. Milton was Latin Secretary to the Council of State, in effect, something like Foreign Minister; he was the great champion, as Williams also was in his lesser sphere, of freedom of

[1] Masson, *Life of Milton*, IV, 528.

religion and of the press; he was a profound scholar
and a skilled linguist. Williams was also a fine linguist,
a researcher into Indian dialects, and had a knowledge
of Dutch, learned in America. He became a frequent
visitor at Milton's house in Petty France, Westminster
(now 19, York Street), where he practised the method
of oral language-teaching by talking Dutch to the
blind scholar and statesman; it was the middle of the
Dutch War, and Milton wanted the language for
official purposes as well as for scholarship. In return
Milton read or talked with Williams in Hebrew, Greek,
Latin, and French. Williams had also two pupils, sons
of a Parliament man, whom he taught by the oral
method, 'as we teach our children English, by words,
phrases and constant talk.'[1]   Sir Henry Vane, too, had
not forgotten his old friends in New England.   Williams
spent ten weeks at Vane's country house, Belleau, in
Lincolnshire, where Lady Vane entertained him while
Sir Henry had to be in London on State business. He
often visited Hugh Peters at Westminster, and apparently had several interviews with Cromwell. He
left England in 1654, with an assurance from Cromwell,
now Lord Protector of England, that Rhode Island
should not be molested by the other New England
colonies. Williams still had an active career before
him as chief magistrate and man of affairs of Rhode
Island, but he never visited England again.

In the second half of the seventeenth century the
number of Americans who came to Great Britain was
somewhat greater than in the first half.   The colonies

[1] From a letter of Williams, quoted by Masson, *op. cit.*, IV, 531.

continued regularly to maintain agents or representatives in London; and occasional deputations came to state grievances or to answer questions before the Privy Council. John Winthrop, Junior, born at his father's manor, Groton in Suffolk, England, was one of the founders of Connecticut. He revisited England in 1641, and then went back to Connecticut. He returned to London in 1662, in order to obtain a charter for his colony. As a cousin of Sir George Downing, and a friend of Lord Say and Sele, one of the patrons of Connecticut, he was well received at Court. He is said to have presented Charles II with a ring which the martyred Charles I gave the elder John Winthrop. He had a successful sojourn in England, obtaining a liberal charter for Connecticut and the incorporation of New Haven in that colony, and was elected a member of the recently founded Royal Society, now the most celebrated and influential of scientific academies. In 1675 he returned to Boston, Massachusetts, and died there in 1676.

After the Revolution of 1688, social relations between England and the colonies were a little closer or rather a little less distant, as trade and commerce were making progress. The intellectual life of New England, which was to rise to wonderful splendour, was beginning to be recognised in England in the opening years of the eighteenth century. The eminent Massachusetts family of Mather was well known in England. Richard Mather, a Congregational clergyman, had gone out from Bristol to Massachusetts in 1635. His youngest son, Increase, was born at Dorchester near Boston in

1639. Increase became a Master of Arts, Fellow, and President of Harvard. He also graduated at Trinity College, Dublin (1658), where his eldest brother, Samuel, English-born, was a Fellow. Increase served for a time as minister at Great Torrington in Devon and remained in England until 1661. The High Anglican churchmanship of the Restoration proved too much for him to accept, so, like many other ministers of religion, he gave up his living. Returning to Massachusetts, he became pastor at the North Church, Boston, in 1664, and continued, much beloved, in this office for nearly sixty years. In 1684 he was elected President of Harvard College. In 1688 he was sent to England to defend the liberties of Massachusetts (its charter having been cancelled) and had an audience with James II. He received a gracious reception, but formed the impression that the monarch only wanted to be rid of him. After the flight of James, he had a satisfactory interview with the successor-king, William of Orange. The Revolution had changed the face of English politics, so there was little difficulty in obtaining the restoration of the Massachusetts charter. Early in the next century (1713) his learned son, Cotton Mather, the defender of witch-hanging, was elected a Fellow of the Royal Society of London after he had corresponded frequently with it. He appears never to have visited England. In the same election the Royal Society honoured Thomas Brattle, a Boston merchant. He was a graduate of Harvard, and a benefactor of that college; he was also Treasurer of Harvard for the last twenty years of his life. He was elected to the

Royal Society because of the accounts of eclipses which from time to time he had sent to it; like Cotton Mather he appears to have been elected in absence.[1]

[1] Cotton Mather's scientific communications to the Royal Society have been reprinted from the American Antiquarian Society (Worcester, Massachusetts). They comprise letters concerning the flora and fauna of North America. Thomas Brattle is not mentioned in the printed lists of the Royal Society, but I am informed by the Librarian that he is in the Society's records.

II

BENJAMIN FRANKLIN IN ENGLAND

In 1724 there came to London from Philadelphia a youth of eighteen, who was to be one of the greatest of the Americans, and who, on three successive visits, was altogether to spend sixteen and a half years in England. It is a natural mistake to consider that as Franklin was so exceptional a man, the familiarity which he established for himself in England was an exceptional thing. This was not so. Sailings from the American colonies to England, if not exactly regular, were frequent, and passages were easily obtained. The well-to-do travelled in the cabin, those with small means in the steerage which is described briefly but graphically in *The Journal of John Woolman.* The many-sided eighteenth century was an age of cosmopolitanism. Never before had individuals moved about so much and taken root so easily for long or for short periods, in one country or another. Voltaire, Rousseau, Leibniz, and numerous generals, admirals, and Prime Ministers who served alien governments, are instances of this citizenship of the world, which was not incompatible with a real and lofty patriotism. Of the citizens of the world Franklin is the perfect example. Nobody will challenge the breadth of his sympathy, the light of his intelligence, the zest of his curiosity; nor yet, on the other hand, will they deny that this good citizen of the world was one of the greatest of Americans, one of the most public-spirited, loyal, patriotic. 'Far more a "good European," a citizen of the world, than Adams or Jefferson, Washington or Hutchinson, he remained to the end more pungently American than any of them.'[1]

Franklin's *Autobiography*, one of the most charming pieces of personal writing in all literature, one of the most *naïve*, serene, and informing, shows the essential unity of English and colonial society in the early eighteenth century. He grew up in New England, in a social environment and with an education such as might have been the lot of a son of a nonconformist family of similar fortune in Old England. The *Autobiography* has painted the picture of such a family: The serious and hard-working father and mother, and the thirteen surviving children, all seated together round the table in the small Boston house; the elder brothers going out, one by one, apprenticed to different trades; the grammar-school education, broken off short, in order that the father should have the youngest son's youthful assistance in his own trade; the impulse of the son to go to sea — an impulse, however, suppressed in face of parental opposition, the boy finding his 'outlet' in boating and swimming with a company of other

[1] Carl Becker in *The Dictionary of American Biography* (1931), VI, 596.

youths, whom he leads into many scrapes around
Boston Harbour. He reads every pamphlet and book
on which he can lay hands; his mind is particularly
impressed by Greenwood's *English Grammar*, Locke's
Essay on Human Understanding, and du Port Royal's
Art of Thinking. Benjamin becomes apprentice to his
brother who is a printer, proves too clever for the
brother, sells his books to raise a little money, and goes
off to seek his living by himself. He lands in Philadelphia with one Dutch dollar in his pocket, and obtains
work with a printer. He has serious thoughtful friends,
attracts the attention of the Governor.

When Franklin sailed to England in 1724, he was in
the cabin with the wealthy passengers, and lived
'uncommonly well,' in a very sociable company.
Arriving in the Thames on December 24, 1724, he
took lodgings in 'Little Britain,' at three shillings and
sixpence a week. He had just fifteen pistoles in his
pocket, but at once found work in Palmer's Printing-
Office, Bartholomew Close.

The first visit of Franklin to England lasted about
eighteen months, December 24, 1724, to June 23, 1726.
The work of composition in the printing-room was
arduous, but interesting; for instance when he had to
set up Wollaston's *Religion of Nature*. Disagreeing
with some of Wollaston's arguments, the young printer
wrote and printed a pamphlet on *Liberty and Necessity,
Pleasure and Pain*. He made friends with a bookseller,
and for a small payment was allowed to borrow any of
the books. He drank only water, and swam in the
Thames — Chelsea to Blackfriars (four miles) being one

of his longest swims. His fellow workmen drank large quantities of beer, pathetically believing that this kept them strong; it cost them five shillings of their weekly wages (which were, apparently, about thirty shillings), and only muddled their brains and bodies. 'Thus these poor devils keep themselves always under,' wrote Franklin. In July, 1726, he took passage from Gravesend, feeling the call of Pennsylvania. He had not improved his fortune in London, but 'had picked up some very ingenious acquaintance,' and 'had read considerably.'

There are some people so vivid that their whole life is romantic and thrilling; of this band was Benjamin Franklin. After his return to Philadelphia, England did not see him again for thirty-one years, and these were filled with incessant and responsible labours and stimulating experiences. Printing, editing, writing, municipal and state politics engaged his attention and absorbed some of his activity. He made experiments in electricity and was elected, in absence, a Fellow of the Royal Society of London. He assisted the unfortunate and brave General Braddock to find transport for the fatal expedition into the wilds of Northern Pennsylvania. In 1757 the Colony of Pennsylvania sent him to England to present the case for taxing the land of the Penn family, on account of the expenses of defence against the French and Indians. He was then fifty-one years old. He took his son (afterwards Royalist Governor of New Jersey) with him; they landed at Falmouth on July 17, and made their way to London by easy stages, visiting, as they went,

Stonehenge, Salisbury, and Lord Pembroke's house
and gardens at Wilton. At the end of the journey
Franklin wrote home to his wife;

To Mrs. Deborah Franklin.

London, July 27, 1757.

My dear Child,

We arrived here well last night, only a little fatigued,
the last day's journey being 70 miles.

Mistress Deborah was not highly educated, and had
never been an intellectual companion to him. They
were, however, fond of each other, although Mrs.
Franklin's affection was not sufficient to make her
eager to face the journey over the Atlantic with him;
nor, indeed, though he would have liked to have his
wife with him, did Franklin feel the temporary separation very acutely. He would not, however (he wrote
to her) contemplate a permanent settlement in England, 'because of your invincible aversion to crossing
the seas.' He wrote letters to Mrs. Franklin frequently
and affectionately, and he testifies that she too, on
her side, was a most faithful correspondent. She advised
him to take care of his health; and acting on her counsel,
he decided to keep his own chariot in London, because
whenever he went out he caught a fresh cold. He sent
presents to her from time to time, the sort of things
that a woman likes: various knick-knacks and useful
things for the home — English china, a piece of carpet-
ing for the best room, snuffers, 'a pair of silk blankets,
very fine,' four pocket-handkerchiefs out of eight which
he had just purchased. She sends him a Nocake which
he finds 'very good.' He tells her about the expenses

of living in London, and how his income is reduced through the expiring of his printing-partnership with Mr. Hall at home. Nevertheless he is able to assure her: 'For my own Part, I live here as frugally as possible, not to be destitute of the Comforts of Life, making no dinners for anybody, and contenting myself with a single Dish when I dine at home; and yet such is the dearness of Living here in every Article, that my Expenses amaze me. I see, too, by the sums you have received in my absence, that yours are very great.'[1] The most philosophical of husbands are always surprised at the amount which it costs to keep up the home when the money is not being spent upon themselves.

The five years which Franklin spent in England on this, his second, visit, were probably the happiest in his life.[2] The want of his own domestic circle was supplied by the family of his landlady, Mrs. Margaret Stevenson, of 7, Craven Street, London. The agent of Philadelphia, the eminent scholar, kindly, cheerful, wise, raised above youthful passion in a serene and vigorous middle-age, was like an elder brother, uncle or godfather, to the family at 7, Craven Street, loving and beloved. Besides this congenial domestic circle, he had exactly the kind of society which he enjoyed outside home: the conversation of scholars, members of scientific societies; the debates in the House of Commons; conferences with statesmen on matters of high policy. His political mission for the Colony of Pennsylvania

[1] *Writings* (edited by Smyth, 1907), V, 32. This letter was written towards the end of the English visit, June 22, 1767.

[2] Carl Becker, *op. cit.*, 589.

BENJAMIN FRANKLIN

fared well enough, though slowly. In 1760 the Privy Council conceded the claim of the Pennsylvania Assembly, and King George III allowed a bill for the taxation of the Penn family estates like those of other landowners. The business of missions like this of Franklin's always proceeds slowly, with many and long interruptions or intervals. He had plenty of time to pursue his social and scientific activities; life was busy, useful, tranquil, conducive to reflection, to wise conversation, to original experiment, to a widespread literary correspondence.

Franklin's chief friends in London were the scientists Collinson and Fothergill, the philosopher Priestley, and the member of Parliament, William Strahan. Peter Collinson, a man of ample means, interested in botany and physics, had sent valuable presents in 1730 to the Subscription Library which Franklin was then helping to found. For more than thirty years after this, Collinson acted as the unpaid agent in London for choosing and purchasing and shipping books for the Philadelphia Library. In 1745 he sent over to the Philosophical Society of Philadelphia an account of recent German experiments in electricity, together with a glass tube and directions for using it. The result of this was a fruitful series of experiments by Franklin, and letters on electricity written by him to Collinson which were published, and translated into most European languages. Collinson lived at Mill Hill, in Middlesex, near London, until his death at the age of seventy-five in 1768. Priestley was then a Congregational minister at Nantwich. He carried on experiments in electricity and made friends with Franklin during a visit to London. Besides personal association with these and other men of science, Franklin corresponded with the Scottish philosophers David Hume and Lord Kames, and also with Dr. Johnson, whom, however, although they were both resident in London, he appears never to have met. Alongside of an active correspondence with eminent men, Franklin gave useful and friendly advice to his young friends. On May 16, 1760, he sends to his 'good girl,' Miss Stevenson, at Wansted, a letter of advice on reading, along with a present of books in French, dealing with 'philosophic and practical knowledge.'

I would advise you to read with a pen in your hand, and enter in a little book short hints of what you find that is curious or that may be useful; for this will be the best method of imprinting such particulars in your memory, where they will be ready, either for practice on some future occasion, if they are matters of utility, or at least to adorn and improve your conversation, if they are rather points of curiosity. And as many of the terms of science are such as you cannot have met with in your common reading, and may therefore be unacquainted with, I think it would be well for you to have a good dictionary at hand, to consult immediately when you meet with a word you do not comprehend the precise meaning of. This may at first seem troublesome and interrupting; but it is a trouble that will daily diminish, as you will daily find less and less occasion for your dictionary, as you become more acquainted with the terms; and in the meantime you will read with more satisfaction, because with more understanding. When any point occurs, in which you would be glad to have further information than your book affords you, I beg you would not in the least apprehend, that I should think it a trouble to receive and answer your questions. It will be a pleasure and no trouble. For though I may not be able, out of my own little stock of knowledge, to afford you what you require, I can easily direct you to the books where it may most rapidly be found. Adieu, and believe me ever, my dear friend,

Yours affectionately
B. FRANKLIN

There was nothing upon which Franklin's mind could not exercise itself with interest and originality; and his sound judgment was always available for his friends on any subject, whether it was on the best kind of physical exercise, or the desirability of early marriage, or improvements in type-casting. One of his best letters was written (1760) to John Baskerville, the celebrated designer and founder of type. In addition to his correspondence, conducted from Craven Street, he had his experimental electrical machine there, and also composed a humorous *Craven Street Gazette*, chronicling the proceedings of Royalty for the amusement of the Stevenson family. He had means and leisure for occasional travel, and visited Cambridge and the home of his ancestors at Ecton; he also made a journey to Scotland. Scottish society, as described in the *Reminiscences* of Alexander Carlyle of Inveresk was at this time highly cultured, philosophical, hospitable, and convivial. Franklin stayed with Sir Alexander Dick, who was President of the College of Physicians, Edinburgh, at Prestonfield, a pleasant house and estate outside the city. Here he spent a most agreeable time and made warm friends. This tour, towards the end of 1759, included some weeks in Yorkshire and Lincolnshire and covered fifteen hundred miles. Franklin also went abroad to Holland, and studied the insurance system by which people were encouraged to save for an independent old age. St. Andrews University and Oxford conferred on him their doctor's degree. At Ecton in 1758 he saw his grandfather's grave, searched the parish register as far as it went back (to 1555), and traced the births, marriages, and deaths of Franklins throughout the period down to his own time. He found that for five generations back his line was 'the youngest son of a youngest son.' For hundreds of years the family had the business of a smith, the elder son being always trained to that craft.

This citizen of the world, this essential man of the eighteenth century, like Voltaire had a loathing of war, and put forward means of common sense for preventing it. One of his ideas, later adopted with excellent results by the United States, was for the transfer of territory by agreed purchase.[1] During his second residence in England, the Seven Years' War was in progress, and he followed its course with lively interest. When, with the accession of George III in 1760, a powerful movement was started from the Court in favour of peace, Franklin, like Pitt, thought the design premature. He published in the London *Chronicle* a satire on *The Meanes of Disposing the Ennemie to Peace*.[2] Though he liked the people in England, he did not believe that peace at this moment was being demanded by the

[1] Project for Preventing War (1788), in *Memoirs of B. Franklin*, edited by W. T. Franklin (1819), VI, 137.

[2] *Writings*, IV, 90 ff.

soundest elements but by certain other classes who wanted peace: for instance, 'All those who be timorous by Nature, amongst whom may be reckoned Men of Learning that lead sedentary lives, using little Exercise of Body, and thence obtaining but few and weake Spirits; Great Statesmen, whose natural spirits be exhausted by much thinking; together with all Women, whose Power, weake as they are, is not a little amongst the Menne; these shall incessantly speake for Peace; and finally all Courtiers, who suppose they conform thereby to the Inclinations of the Prince.'

When the question arose whether Canada should be retained, or exchanged for Guadeloupe, Franklin again was on the side of Pitt, and published an essay pointing out the advantages which Canada would bring to the British Empire. Sugar islands, he argued, were highly overrated. People should realise that they were paying not only the market price per pound, but the cost of the wars waged for the island and of armies and navies employed in protecting them. Besides, the blood of the slaves who were torn from their African homes to cultivate sugar, and the blood of the soldiers and sailors shed for the islands, was enough to make all the sugar 'thoroughly dyed red.'

Canada, on the other hand, according to Franklin's theories of population (he anticipated the views of Malthus), being a country of almost limitless land and sources of food, would rapidly increase the number of its people who, however, would always remain agricultural and therefore would not compete with the manufacturers of Britain. Besides, Canada, a con-

tinental American region, would, if transferred to Great
Britain, threaten no other Power, for there was none
near it; and, from the point of view of the interests
of the Thirteen American Colonies, Canada in British
hands would help to solve the problem of defence
against the Indians. 'Canada, in the hands of Britain,
will endanger the kingdom of France as little as any
other cession; and from its situation and circumstances
cannot be hurtful to any other state.' The American
Colonies want Canada. Forts are not sufficient to pro-
tect them from Indians. 'When they have surpriz'd
separately, and murdered and scalped a dozen families,
they are gone with inconceivable expedition, through
unknown ways, and 'tis very rare that pursuers have
any chance of coming up with them. In short, long
experience has taught our planters that they cannot
rely upon forts as a security against *Indians*: The inhabitants of *Hackney* might as well rely upon the tower
of *London* to secure them against highwaymen and
housebreakers.'[1] Franklin's views are believed to have
influenced the British Government in the peace terms
which it finally arranged with France in 1762.

He outstayed his original official mission in England
after the dispute concerning the Penn estates was
settled in 1760, for some further colonial business de-
tained him during another two years. He thoroughly
enjoyed English life, and thought of going back to

[1] 'The Interest of Great Britain Considered with regard to her Colonies
and the Acquisition of Canada and Guadeloupe, to which are added Observations concerning the Interest of Mankind, Peopling of Countries, etc.'
Writings, IV, 32, 40, 43; see also Carl Becker, *Dictionary of American Biography*, s.v. *Franklin*.

America only in order to make arrangements for a permanent return to England. 'In two years at far-thest, I hope to settle all my Affairs in such a Manner, as that I *May* then conveniently remove to England — provided that we can persuade the good Woman to cross the Seas.'[1]   In August, 1762, he reluctantly took ship to Philadelphia and from there wrote to the Stevenson family in London a letter of poignant regret.

> Of all the enviable Things England has, I envy it most its People. Why should that petty Island, which compared to America is but like a stepping-stone in a Brook, scarce enough of it above Water to keep one's shoes dry; why, I say, should that little Island enjoy in almost every Neigh-bourhood, more sensible virtuous and elegant Minds, than we can collect in ranging 100 Leagues of our vast Forests? But 'tis said the Arts delight to Travel Westward. You have effectually defended us in this glorious War, and in time you will improve us.[2]

In two years Franklin was back again in England, having embarked from Chester on the Delaware on November 7, 1764, and landed at Portsmouth on December 9. He went to London and took up his old quarters at 7, Craven Street, much to the delight of the Stevenson family. His mission on this visit was to obtain the cancellation of the Pennsylvania Charter, so that a final settlement could be made of the disputes with the Penn family. This object was not attained, and the question was forgotten or merged in the tre-mendous controversy over the Stamp Act. On this,

---

[1] To William Strahan, from Philadelphia, Dec. 7, 1762, *Writings*, IV, 182.

[2] *Writings*, IV, 194 (to Miss Mary Stevenson, March 25, 1763), from Philadelphia.

his third and last visit, Franklin stayed for eleven
years. Naturally, this time of political stress made it
impossible for him to lead the life of the leisured philosopher, scientist, and man of the world which he had
enjoyed so much on his second visit. He had now to
immerse himself in political affairs, labouring in the
interests not simply of his own colony, but of all the
Thirteen Colonies and also of the British Empire which
he wished to see united and intact. He had his English
friends, however, and was an object of curiosity and
respectful interest on the part of the public. It was at
Twyford, the country house of the 'good bishop,'
Dr. Shipley of St. Asaph, 'expecting the enjoyment of
a week's uninterrupted leisure,' that he began to com-
pose in 1771 the justly celebrated *Autobiography*.

There was not much leisure, however, for the most
famous American statesman in England at that critical
time. He was 'explaining, consulting, disputing, in a
continual hurry from morning till night.' He opposed,
when consulted by George Grenville, the plan of passing
the Stamp Bill, but when it became law, he advised the
Americans to make the best of it in a letter of great
beauty.

> The Tide was too strong against us.... We might as well
> have hindered the sun's setting. That we could not do.
> But since 'tis down, my friend, and it may be long before
> it rises again, let us make as good a night of it as we can.
> We may still light candles. Frugality and Industry will
> go a great way towards indemnifying us.[1]

In February, 1766, he underwent a good examination

[1] To Charles Thomson, from London, July 11, 1765; *Writings*, IV, 390.

before the Committee of the Whole House of Commons, and answered 174 questions about the Stamp Act, which, he argued, was contrary to constitutional custom and was administratively impracticable. The last questions and answers were:

Q. What used to be the pride of the Americans?
A. To indulge in the fashions and manufactures of Great Britain.
Q. What is now their pride?
A. To wear their old cloaths over again, till they can make new ones.[1]

Franklin's strenuous and statesmanlike efforts to deal fairly with both parties to the dispute were not given the credit which they deserved.

I do not find that I have gained any point, in either country, except that of rendering myself suspected by my impartiality; in England of being too much of the American, and in America, of being too much an Englishman.[2]

Until the passing of the Coercive Acts in 1774 'he never quite despaired.' He gave it as his opinion that the Pennsylvanians were not so very badly off under their proprietary system, in spite of the absenteeism of the Penn family. 'Even this Capitol [sic], the residence of the King, is now a daily scene of lawless riot and confusion.' He thought that the British people were preparing a judgment for themselves: 'What the event will be, God only knows. But some punishment

[1] *The Examination of Doctor Benjamin Franklin etc. in the British House of Commons, relative to the Repeal of the American Stamp Act, 1765; Writings*, IV, 412–48.
[2] *Writings*, V, 182. To an unknown correspondent, London, Nov. 28, 1768.

seems preparing for a people, who are ungratefully abusing the best constitution and the best King any nation was ever blessed with, intent on nothing but luxury, licentiousness, power, places, pensions and plunder.' [1] He had frequent talks with Chatham on the American question, at Chatham's house, Hayes in Kent, and at Number 7, Craven Street; and he wrote a wise satire: *Rules by which a great Empire may be reduced to a small one.*[2] In spite of the affair of the Hutchinson letters and the furious onslaught of Solicitor-General Wedderburn upon him as the 'Man of Three Letters' (*fur*, thief), on January 29, 1774, he remained in England until March 21, 1775, when he took ship from Portsmouth for Philadelphia. He would have liked well enough to stay in England; his means were amply sufficient for this purpose.

> I have indeed so many good kind Friends here, that I could spend the remainder of my Life among them with great Pleasure, if it were not for my American connections, and the indelible Affection for that dear Country, from which I have been so long in a State of Exile.[3]

He had still a balance of money left behind in England. On June 27, 1775, he wrote from Philadelphia, entrusting the care of this property to John Sargent, M.P. for Seaford.

> It may possibly soon be all I shall have left, as my American Property consists chiefly of houses in our Seaport Towns, which your Ministry have begun to burn,

---

[1] *Writings*, V, 133. To John Ross, London, May 14, 1768; Becker, *op. cit.*
[2] *Writings*, VI, 118, 127.
[3] *Writings*, V, 382. To William Franklin, January 30, 1772.

and I suppose are wicked enough to burn them all. It now requires great Wisdom on your Side the Water to prevent a total Separation; I hope it will be found among you. We shall give you one Opportunity more of recovering our Affairs and retaining the Connection; and that I fear will be the last.[1]

The chance passed away. The separation came and with it a separation of hearts. William Strahan and Franklin had been old and good friends; but on July 5, 1775, the American wrote from Philadelphia:

Mr. Strahan

You are a Member of Parliament, and one of that majority which has doomed my Country to Destruction. — You have begun to burn our Towns, and murder our People. — Look upon your Hands. They are stained with the Blood of your Relations! — You and I were long Friends: — You are now my Enemy and I am
                              Yours
                                        B. FRANKLIN

This was a terrible letter, the cutting off of old ties, the outpouring of an indignant heart. But the old philosopher would not let the sun go down on his wrath; the letter was never sent.

[1] *Writings*, VI, 407.

III

THE AMERICAN REVOLUTION

In the cosmopolitan eighteenth century men changed their homes and countries easily. The Americans, however, in their own country, largely removed from the cosmopolitan influence of Europe, developed a strongly local point of view, so that it is difficult to realise how the separate colonies ever became 'a United States.' They were not great travellers. Probably the expenses of travel through France, Germany, and Italy were beyond their means. Residence in England, however, was possible; and all sorts of things drew them to England in the eighteenth century — schools, trade, friends and relatives, religion.

Samuel Johnson, of the class of 1715 at Yale College, first a school-teacher and later a Congregational minister in Connecticut, felt doubts about the conditions of his ministry. As there were no Anglican bishops in America before the Revolution, he went to England to seek orders. In 1723 he was ordained in the Anglican communion. He visited Alexander Pope, and was received and appreciated in scholarly circles. In later

life he was President of King's College, New York
(now Columbia University), and was made a Doctor
of Divinity by Oxford University. His friendship with
Bishop Berkeley procured the bequest of Berkeley's
library for Yale, where it still is. Samuel Miller of
Milton, a graduate of Harvard, was sent by the Episcopal congregation of Braintree, Massachusetts, to
Oxford in 1726, where he took the degree of Master of
Arts preparatory to ordination. Then he returned to
Braintree, and was inducted into the Episcopal Church
there on Christmas Day. He remained pastor for
thirty-six years. In 1747 he visited England again and
received the degree of Doctor of Divinity from the
University of Oxford.

On the eve of the Revolution there arrived in England
one of the most gentle souls who have ever expressed
themselves in characteristic journals. John Woolman
was a native of Northampton, Burlington County,
West Jersey. His pious parents made him, before he
was seven years old, 'acquainted with the operations
of divine love.' One day, coming from school, he left
his companions who were playing by the way, and sitting down read the twenty-second chapter of Revela-
tion: 'He showed me a pure river of water of life.' The
place where he sat, and the sweetness that attended his
mind, remained fresh in his memory; in this simple,
pure frame of mind, he lived to the end. At first he
worked on his father's farm, but after the age of twenty-
one, he went into trade, first as a store-clerk, and later
on his own account as a tailor; but his heart was in the
contemplation, prayer, and useful work of the Society

of Friends to which he belonged. All his spare time was spent in journeys, especially to the 'back settlements.' His gentleness and charity made him take note carefully of slavery. Woolman became one of the first of 'Abolitionists.'

When he was about fifty years old, Woolman felt 'a religious concern to prepare for crossing the sea, in order to visit Friends in the northern parts of England, and more particularly in Yorkshire.' Having informed the Friends of this 'religious exercise' which 'attended' his mind, at the Burlington Monthly Meeting, the Quarterly Meeting, and the General Spring Meeting, and having obtained consent and a certificate from all three, he set forth from Chester, Pennsylvania, on May 1, 1772. He travelled in the steerage where the sailors slept, and he pitied their condition. 'If, after having been on deck several hours in the night, they come down into the steerage soaking wet, and are so closely stowed that proper convenience for change of garments is not easily come at, but for want of proper room their wet garments are thrown in heaps, and sometimes, through much crowding, are trodden under foot in going to their lodgings and getting out of them — it is difficult at times for each to find his own. Here are trials for the poor sailors.' During his stay in England he found time to write some essays, including one on 'A Sailor's Life.'

John Woolman landed at London on June 8, 1772. All the way over he had held meetings on the ship, at which the sailors attended. He now, on landing, 'went straightway' to the Yearly Meeting of ministers and elders, which he found already in session. In his haste, he burst into the quiet room, and was taken for a wild enthusiast, and had difficulty in persuading the Friends to give him their approval or 'unity' for the pursuance of his ministry in England. The Yearly Meeting in London lasted for a week, morning and afternoon; John Woolman felt his mind 'enlarged' in the sessions. On June 15, he went to the Quarterly Meeting at Hertford, Sherrington, Northampton, Banbury, and Shipton, with other 'sundry meetings between,' to Warwick, Coventry, Birmingham, and so northwards through Nottingham and Sheffield, till he reached Settle in Yorkshire. He had no horse, and refused to travel in the stage-coaches, on account of reports of their hard conditions.

Stage-coaches go upwards of one hundred miles in twenty-four hours; and I have heard Friends say in several places that it is common for horses to be killed with hard driving, and that many others are driven till they go blind. Post-boys pursue their business, each one to his stage, all night through the winter. Some boys who ride long stages suffer greatly in winter nights, and at several places I have heard of their being frozen to death. So great is the hurry in the spirit of this world, that in aiming to do business quickly and to gain wealth, the creation at this day doth loudly groan.

As he went along, Woolman enquired about prices and wages. Wheat was eight shillings a bushel, or sixty-four shillings a quarter (in the Napoleonic Wars it rose to one hundred and twenty shillings; in 1934 it was as low as twenty shillings). Mutton was threepence to fivepence a pound, bacon sevenpence to ninepence, cheese fourpence to sixpence, butter eightpence to tenpence. Wood for fires was 'very scarce and dear'; coal two shillings and sixpence a hundredweight, except near the pits where it was not a quarter so much. Wages of labourers in the Home Counties (around London) were tenpence a day, the employer finding small beer; in harvest-time, the wages were a shilling a day, the employer at this season also finding the labourer in food.

> Industrious women who spin in the factories get some fourpence, some fivepence, and so on to six, seven, eight, nine or ten pence per day, and find their own house-room and diet. Great numbers of poor people live chiefly on bread and water in the southern parts of England, as well as in the northern parts, and there are many poor children not even taught to read. May those who have abundance lay these things to heart.

Woolman must have felt somewhat cut off from his friends, for he would not send letters by the stage-coaches, and he had asked his correspondents both in England and, before he sailed, in America, to refrain from sending letters by the stage-post. He had also great distress of mind on account of Friends whose business was connected, even if only indirectly, with the slave trade. In general he was afraid that Friends were not seeing things clearly; they should dig deep and cast forth superfluous matter and 'get down to the rock.'

In the Lake District, near Kendal, he stayed with a Friend, Jane Crossman, 'who was once in America.' Shortly afterwards he heard that his kinsman, William Hunt of North Carolina, who was on a visit to the

Friends in England, had died of smallpox in New-castle. Woolman himself was feeling weak from his long walks, often in wet weather, over muddy roads, and amid offensive smells. In September he fell ill of smallpox at York. On October 5 (1772), this minister of the 'Prince of Peace' went forth on his last journey, into the unknown. In the part of his journal covering the whole of his time in England, he makes not the faintest allusion to the dispute between England and the colonies.

All the Americans who came to England in the years before the Revolutionary War seem, like Franklin, and even the unworldly and uncompromising Wool-man, to have felt themselves at home. They were either agents for the colonies (although the agencies were in many cases held by Englishmen, like Edmund Burke, agent for New York, 1770-74); or they were merchants, clever young men who became junior partners in some established English house trading with the colonies; or they were youths sent, chiefly from Virginia, to school at Eton or Westminster; or they were simply visitors, like Thackeray's *Virginian* or *Richard Carvel*, who came to England to see it and to stay for a while. Some of them stood for English constituencies and were elected to Parliament. It has been ascertained that there were no Americans elected to the Parliament of 1761, but that five sat in the House of Commons between 1763 and 1783.[1] They all came from the northern colonies: John Huske, M.P. for Malden, 1763-73, from New Hampshire; Paul

[1] L. B. Namier, *England in the Age of the American Revolution* (1930), 267.

Wentworth, M.P. for Saltash, 1780, from New Hampshire; Barlow Trecothick, M.P. for the City of London, 1768–74, from Massachusetts; Henry Cruger, M.P. for Bristol, 1774–80, from New York; Staats Long Morris, M.P. for Elgin Burghs, 1774–84, from New York. Three were merchants. Wentworth was an agent of the British Government. Morris, a brother of Gouverneur Morris, was an officer in the army. William Lee of Virginia, a merchant and agent for Virginia, stood, without success, for Southwark, as a Whig, in 1774. Those who sent their sons and their daughters for education to England were mainly Southerners, especially Carolinians. The four men who signed the Declaration of Independence on behalf of South Carolina had all been educated in England. They were Thomas Lynch,[1] Eton, Caius College, Cambridge, and the Inner Temple; E. Rutledge, Inner Temple; Arthur Middleton, Westminster School; Thomas Hayward, Middle Temple. East Apthorp was elected a Fellow of Jesus College, Cambridge, in 1758. He had been sent over from Boston as a boy to be educated and had been placed in charge of an English merchant, John Thomlinson, agent for New Hampshire, who, after seeing to the education of the youth, obtained the support of the Duke of Newcastle in an application for a Fellowship.

The life of the Americans in England before the Revolutionary War has been described in Peter van Schaack's diary, by Samuel Curwen, and from references in contemporary Englishmen's letters and diaries. Those who came merely for a visit lived in

[1] The facts in the above paragraph are from Namier, *op. cit.*, 267, 290.

London in lodgings, attended the play and the coffee-houses, took coach and went to see their friends and relatives in the country. The merchants and colonial agents who were more or less permanent residents in London had their particular coffee-houses, the clubs of those days; there was a 'New York Coffee-house,' a 'Carolina Coffee-house,' a 'New England Coffee-house,' and others.[1] On the day of the repeal of the Stamp Act (March 11, 1766) the lobby of the House of Commons, the Court of Requests, and the avenues were blocked with American merchants, although most of them may have been Englishmen trading with America.[2]

Even during the Revolutionary War there were a good many Americans in England, most of them Tories, no doubt, who on the whole disapproved of the American cause; others had no very strong opinions one way or the other. So long as they kept their opinions to themselves they were not troubled by the British Government. The New England Coffee-house in Threadneedle Street remained open, and took in the New York newspapers for its *clientèle* to read. Some of this *clientèle* were active 'Loyalists,' but not all.

There was a certain Samuel Curwen, one of the ineffective Hamlets who are a feature of every time of trouble. He was called a Tory (though he denied the fairness of the epithet). He had no sympathy for the Revolution, but not because he was a convinced upholder of the Crown on principle. He was a quiet and

---

[1] Namier, *op. cit.*, 291; also, *The Journal and Letters of Samuel Curwen* (1842), 31, 41.

[2] H. Walpole, *The Reign of George III*, II, 212.

careful *bourgeois*, honourable, public-spirited, but not
heroic or adventurous. He had, it is true, his romance
of war and adventure, for he had made the expedition
against Louisbourg with the men of New England in
1744-45, serving with the rank of Captain, but that
was when he was still under thirty. After Louisbourg,
he had carried on his business as a merchant of Salem
and had made money. Later, he held the positions of
Impost Officer for Essex County and Judge of the
Admiralty Court at Salem. He disliked party controversy and took no interest in it, except in so far as he
deplored its waste of time and energy, its interruption
of useful daily work and settled routine; so on May 13,
1775, leaving his wife behind him, he took ship for
London, and remained in England throughout the
whole of the Revolutionary War. He saw that most
people, there, like himself, were not deeply moved by
the principles which either side in the struggle put
forward, but on the whole they backed, or acquiesced
with, the Government, as people who felt like this
naturally would do. He kept a full journal throughout his stay, travelled considerably, living modestly,
but not poorly, on such means as he had brought with
him, and found reasonably pleasant company, both
English and American.

Curwen landed at Dover on July 3, 1775, spent the
night there, and proceeded next day to London, 'arriving at the New England Coffee-house, Threadneedle
Street at 7 o'clock p.m.,' where he met a fellow towns-
man. 'There is an army of New Englanders here,' he
writes; he calls New England 'my country,' and when

the war was over he returned to it, lived long, and died there. He was not altogether at home in Old England, because New England was his country, but he was not repelled. Dr. Johnson, who said, 'I am willing to think well of all mankind except an American,' was not typical of the attitude of the Englishmen of the Revolutionary period.

In general the English are a tranquil and tolerant race. 'America furnishes matter for disputes in the coffee-houses,' writes Curwen on August 31, 1775 (this was four months and a half after the skirmish at Lexington). 'It is unfashionable,' however (he adds), 'and even disreputable to look askew on one another for differences of opinion in political matters; the doctrine of toleration, if not better understood, is, thank God, better practised here than in America.' He came to the conclusion that men of influence on either side of the Atlantic did 'not understand the real interest of Great Britain and the colonies.' According to his observations, 'the upper ranks, most of the capital stockholders, and, I am told, the principal nobility, are forcing supremacy of parliament over the colonies, and from the middle classes downward are opposed to it.' This statement seems to imply that a numerical majority of the country was not in favour of the Government's American policy; yet Curwen writes almost on the same page: 'The opposition in Parliament is too inconsiderable in numbers, weight and measures to hinder the progress of the administration in their plans respecting America.' The members of the House of Commons, it is true, were drawn from a very small electorate, yet in all great national crises, in the time of William III, Chatham, and George III, they seem fairly to have represented the general sense of the country.

On April 7, 1777, Curwen, who was then travelling over England, noted in his journal: 'You will scarce meet one that entertains the least shadow of a doubt that Government must succeed in the utmost extent of its views before the Fall.' After Saratoga, however, although the Court went on saying *delenda est Carthago*, the old politicians, neither biassed by hatred of America nor interested in the destruction of the colonies, 'shake their heads at this language.'

Curwen stayed in England (using the New England Coffee-house as his club all the time) throughout the war-period and for about a year after peace was made. He sailed for home in August, 1784, taking with him a collection of books which he had been purchasing in England for the social library in Salem. During the last part of his time in England the Government gave him £100 a year, which was probably about the equivalent of his lost salary or fees as Impost Officer of Essex County and Judge of the Salem Admiralty Court. On returning to Massachusetts he seems to have recovered his property and business, for he lived tranquilly, and apparently respected, dying at Salem in 1802 at the age of eighty-six.

The England which Samuel Curwen saw during his nine years' sojourn there was not exactly the England of Dr. Johnson. Curwen was not a man of letters; he does not mention Johnson, or Boswell, or the literary clubs. Curwen's England, though engaged in war with the colonies, was really an England of the Americans. He consorted with Americans, or the English friends (and they seem to have been numerous) of Americans, all the time. He scarcely approved of London, for an early note in his journal is: 'the dissipation, self-forgetfulness and vicious indulgences of every kind which characterise the metropolis, are not to be wondered at.' There was too much wealth for men, weak and subject to temptation. He seems to have passed most afternoons and evenings at the New England Coffee-house, talking, and reading the New York papers. One night, perhaps many nights, he dined with 'eleven New Englanders' at the St. Clement's Coffee-house.

Before the year 1775 was out, he founded a New England Club at the Adelphi Tavern, with a weekly dinner. The Americans in London all seemed to have lived in or near the Adelphi. The New England Club included Samuel Quincy, Harrison Gray, John Clark, Daniel Silsbee, William Cabot, John Singleton Copley, Nathaniel Coffin, Judge Robert Auchmuty, and Governor Hutchinson. British officials who had served in America, or were specially interested in America, dined occasionally at the club. Curwen met Sir Francis Bernard there in February, 1776. As many as twenty-five men would sometimes be at the dinner. He does not seem to have witnessed any of the debates in Parliament, but he saw something of the general election of the year 1776. It was a venal affair, indicating 'the high expectations derivable from a seat in that assembly of untutored, inexperienced youths (for, half, I believe, have not seen thirty), called the parliament of Great Britain.' Being something of a lawyer, he visited the law courts, and admired the carefulness of the British judges; but the noise, he wrote, 'was much greater than would be allowed in our American courts.' He also went to the British Museum and to the Chapter House of Westminster Abbey, where he was shown the authentic Domesday Book and was able to read some of it, in spite of what he ingenuously called its difficult contractions.

London, however, did not hold Curwen continuously. In the summer of 1776, starting in July, he took a journey into the South Midlands and West Country. First he went to Salisbury, and out to Old Sarum, which was as notorious then as it is in the schoolbooks now: 'about sixty acres, unless I am misinformed, without one house on it, and now entitled to send two members to Parliament.' After Old Sarum came Stonehenge. It was a game in those days to count the stones. Curwen, like everybody else, counted several times, and arrived each time at a different total — as if the presiding Druid 'confounds the minds of all who make the iniquitous attempt.' Birmingham (this was before the famous Industrial Revolution) 'in its general appearance looks more like Boston than any place in England.' By September 17 he was in Bristol. There he met a Mr. Eveleigh, a native of Charleston, South Carolina, 'schooled at Cambridge (Massachusetts) under Master Coolidge, and boarded at the President's house. He and his family are hearty in the cause of America.' He also met Harrison Gray, son of the late Massachusetts treasurer; together they went up to

Mr. Gouldney's house at Clifton and saw a wonderful grotto (still extant).

In 1777 Curwen made a tour to the two Universities. At Trinity, Cambridge, he was shown 'a perfect Egyptian mummy, the flesh like smoked tongue.' He enjoyed (who does not?) the 'delightful walks' on the Backs by the Cam. From Cambridge he went to Oxford, and met a couple of Harvard men who were resident in the University, Dr. Nicholson and Mr. Hamilton. He had one evening in a common-room (apparently with the Christ Church dons), 'hearing many sarcastic speeches concerning our New England follies and absurdities.' Bristol seemed to give him something of the home feeling, for he went there again, in 1777, using during his visit 'the America Coffee-house.' He stayed in Queen's Square, and walked out, five miles, to Dundry village and hill, and enjoyed the view of the Severn. The archæology of the ancient British and Romans was much in vogue then. Curwen took a keen interest in it; Bristol is an excellent centre for this study. He met in this city the celebrated Dean Tucker who had a theory that all colonies were useless and had better be cast off. He also heard the preaching at Bristol of John Wesley who had 'the heavens for his canopy.'

It was unfortunate that Bristol produced the only really unpleasant incident of Curwen's stay in England. A 'vixen' saluted him and his friends as 'damned American rebels.' On the other hand, there were unforgettable things: besides Dean Tucker, Wesley, the view of the Severn, Ancient British camps, he saw at the little Bristol spa called Hotwells a person 'dressed

in green, very like an English country gentleman,' who
(as it was said) was really the Emperor of Germany,
Joseph II of Austria, travelling incognito.

Curwen did much of his travelling on horseback.
Once he rode eighty-three miles in fifteen hours, London
to Salisbury, and from there ninety miles in seventeen
hours to Exeter.

The War of American Independence or the 'Revolutionary War' did not, even while it was going on, completely suspend social intercourse. Some American Tory
Loyalists came over to Great Britain at the time of the
troubles and stayed there throughout the period of the
war. Trumbull the painter, who had served as an
officer in the American army in the first part of the war,
was permitted to come to London to pursue his artistic
studies. Another young American, Elkanah Watson,
who had served with distinction in the American forces,
was able to begin his travels in England before hostilities ceased. He came over in September, 1782, a
little apprehensive about his reception. He experienced
no trouble, however, and noticed no signs of hostility
or of social aversion. He thoroughly enjoyed his visit,
and met many important people — the Duke of
Manchester, Burke, Dr. Priestley, James Watt (who
was 'entirely absorbed in his steam-engine projects').
The American painters Copley and West were friendly
to him. Watson was present in the House of Lords
when George III made a speech on the peace which
had just been concluded. He was quite close to the
king, and could follow every expression on his counte-
nance. He describes George's bearing with interest and

sympathy, and without any hint of criticism or prejudice.[1]

A recent study in the history of Great Britain and
the United States has revealed a remarkable group of
Americans in England during the Revolutionary War.
Those were Americans whose patriotism was for
England or the Empire, and who entered the ancient if
not wholly respected profession of spies.

Dr. Edward Bancroft, a native of Westfield, Massachusetts, had been in England for about ten years when
the Revolutionary War opened. He had made money
in the West Indies, and he lived quietly in London,
pursuing scientific studies. He was a friend of Benjamin Franklin, and like Franklin, he had the honour
of being elected to the Royal Society. When the
Revolutionary War broke out in 1775, Silas Deane,
'the first American diplomatist,' who was sent by
Congress to Paris, invited Bancroft to meet him there,
and gave him much valuable information. Bancroft
then returned to London in order, as he said, to attend
to his private affairs and to keep Deane posted on the
condition of politics and the war from the British side.
In London he entered into relations with the British
Cabinet, and supplied it, in return for payment, with
important information (including news of the secret
Franco-American alliance) which came from Deane in
Paris. It was not a very comfortable situation for
Bancroft, as George III distrusted him, and the British

[1] Elkanah Watson, *Men and Times of the Revolution*, including *Journals of Travels in Europe and America from 1777 to 1842* (1850), 178. For Trumbull, see below, Chapter V.

Post Office watched all his correspondence. Years later, when Deane was ill and starving in London, Bancroft was kind to him, and saved his life.

The secret activities of Bancroft were never known to the American Government. He lived out the rest of his life partly in the United States, partly in Great Britain, tranquilly pursuing his scientific studies. He died at Margate, in England, in 1821.

One of the most remarkable Americans in England during the Revolution was Paul Wentworth, a man of birth and property, and a very fashionable figure in London and in the *salon* life of Paris. He was the ideal gentleman-spy, apparently wholly disinterested, except that he wanted to be made a baronet. He did, it is true, accept a salary of £500 from the British Government, but he insisted upon paying his own expenses, and rather perturbed the kindly Lord North who did not like accepting dangerous services in return for such small remuneration. He was never made a baronet, and had no honourable reward except a seat in 1780 in the House of Commons which he held for only six weeks. He was an absolutely trustworthy spy. Lord North assured King George, who disliked spies, that practically all the reports furnished by Wentworth had proved to be accurate. After the war he went out to a plantation which he possessed in Surinam, and died there in 1793.

A third of this remarkable group of Americans in England was the Reverend John Vardill, Professor in King's College (now Columbia University), New York, and Assistant-Minister of the historic Trinity Church in that city. He was in London when the American Revolution began; and soon he is found established in an office in Whitehall itself and actually in Downing Street, the very heart of British high politics. From this office the reverend gentleman conducted secret service work most skilfully, and, among other achievements, succeeded in arranging for the theft of the complete file of dispatches (March 12 to October 7, 1777) sent from the American Commissioners at Paris for transmission to Congress. The bundle of dispatches was delivered safely to the British Cabinet in London while Congress in Philadelphia, after long weary months of waiting for the ship to arrive, at last received a large dummy file of blank paper. Vardill was rewarded by being nominated, through Royal Warrant, Regius Professor of Divinity in King's College. He was never able, however, to take up the appointment. The British Treasury paid him a small pension and procured for him the benefice of Skirbeck and Fishtoft in Lincolnshire. So he ended his life as a priest of a parish, dying in 1811 at the age of fifty-nine.[1]

[1] An admirable book on the spies and others in England and France during the Revolutionary War has been written by L. Einstein, *Divided Loyalties* (1933), published by Houghton Mifflin Company in the United States and Cobden Sanderson in England.

IV

AFTER THE WAR

THE war was over and the people who were previously united in the British Empire and who were now sundered into two, had to make a new adjustment. Actually, social relations between England and America were not very different after the war from what they were before. 'Upon this arguement, I always make my stand,' wrote David Hartley, one of the Peace Commissioners of 1783, in his report on the Treaty of Versailles, 'that we may proceed to open an intercourse between our two countries, as nearly as possible, to the point of *as we were*.' King George III, in his speech in the House of Lords, delivered on December 5, 1782, said: 'Religion, language, interests and affection may, and I hope will, yet prove a bond of permanent union between the two countries.'

John Adams, when he came to London in 1785, the first American Minister to the Court of St. James's, spoke to the same effect when he was presented to George III, and said: 'I shall esteem myself the happiest of men if I can be instrumental in recommending my country more and more to Your Majesty's royal benevolence, and of restoring an entire esteem, confidence and affection or in better words, the old good humour between people who, though separated by an ocean, and under different governments, have the same language, a similar religion and kindred blood.'

George III was a thorough gentleman and, touched to the quick, answered the American in kind. Speaking under the stress of strong emotion, the king said: 'I wish you, sir, to believe, and that it may be understood in America, that I have done nothing in the late contest but what I thought myself indispensably bound to do, by the duty which I owed to my people. I will be very frank with you. I was the last to consent to the separation; but the separation having been made, and having become inevitable, I have always said, as I say now, that I would be the first to meet the friendship of the United States as an independent Power.'

So the train seemed laid for pleasant social relations, but in fact there was not much that took place. John Adams, in spite of his touching meeting with the king, felt, or imagined that he felt, a certain coldness in society. Later diplomatists, however — Jay, Pinckney, and Gouverneur Morris — made themselves at home, as diplomatists usually manage to do, except in the most desolate spots; and neither London nor Philadelphia (the American capital until 1800) could be called desolate. The French War, however, was bound to restrict travellers, the leisured visitors, men of curiosity, observation, and culture; nevertheless at no time between 1792 and 1815 were Americans completely absent from England. One of the most original and, in some respects, one of the most observant, was Gouverneur Morris.

The American statesmen and high politicians of the late eighteenth century, Washington, Hamilton, Jefferson, Aaron Burr, Monroe, to a less extent Madison and John Adams, were accomplished men of the world. This is especially true of Gouverneur Morris. He was born in 1752 in his father's house, Morrisania, New York, received a good education at King's College, New York, and was called to the New York Bar. During the Revolutionary War he was a member of the Continental Congress, and was responsible for the Instructions drawn up for Franklin as American Minister to the Court of Versailles in 1778. Later, he practised law at Philadelphia, and was a delegate to the Convention which made the American Constitution. He engaged in commercial speculations or investments and made a respectable fortune. This enabled him in 1786 to buy the paternal estate, Morrisania, from his elder brother, Staats Long Morris, who was a general in the British army and had married the Duchess of Gordon.

In December, 1788, Gouverneur Morris sailed from Philadelphia for France, in order to gratify his taste for travelling, and to look after some of his investments in wheat and tobacco contracts. He had lost a leg in a carriage accident eight years before, and for the rest of his life he went about with a plain wooden stump below the knee. Nevertheless he won friends wherever he went, moved in the most fashionable circles, and enjoyed every moment of his active and interesting career.

Morris arrived at Paris about three months before the French Revolution began. He witnessed the meeting of the States General at Versailles on May 5, 1789. He saw the bleeding head of Foulon carried through the streets, and the Bastille in ruins. He was made a member of the aristocratic Valois Club, and attended the *salons* of Madame de Chastellux, Madame de Flahaut, Madame de Beauharnais, Madame de Ségur, Madame de Staël, and others.

In August, 1789, Morris sailed from Dieppe to Brighton on a visit to England. The races at Lewes made post-horses very scarce at this moment in Sussex, so Morris had a slow journey to London. On the way he saw 'no land equal to our best soil in America, and very little as good as our second quality.'

Arriving in London, the first thing which he did was to find a hotel, Froome's, Covent Garden, where he engaged a room for six shillings a day, and one shilling a day for his servant. The second thing, especially necessary for a lame man, was to make a contract for a carriage and horses, at four guineas a week, besides a shilling a day for board wages of the coachman. Another system, which Morris adopted on a later visit to England, was to keep a carriage of his own and to pay a coachman twenty-five shillings a week wages, the coachman to 'find himself everything.' A footman (engaged on the later visit) received eighteen guineas per annum *plus* board wages (probably one shilling a day) and living and a greatcoat.

London in 1789 seemed to be full of friendly people. Richard Penn (descendant of the founder of Pennsylvania) received Morris into his family, and asked the American to make the Penn house his home. He went to the Haymarket Theatre; in the next box was Lady Dunmore whom he had known in America twenty years before this; even then she was 'pretty well advanced,' but she still looked well, with the help of some rouge. He visited Trumbull, the American painter, who had a studio in London; and he saw much of the French refugee aristocrats and was very good and generous to them. He tried to console them by saying that 'all the little commotions — burning castles, etc. — though painful and distressing, are but specks in the great business, and will if they get a good constitution soon be forgotten.' English society was quite friendly, but he found the prevailing manners stiff; nor did he like the cooking or wine, neither of which was as good as in France. He thought nothing of 'a composition called turtle soup,' and of another composition supplied to him, called claret. Nevertheless he enjoyed London society and found himself, perhaps to his surprise, very agreeably occupied. He did not come across any signs of animosity among the English against the United States, although he was told that the mere name of America terrified the merchants, they were so afraid of risking money there. Yet there was a well-known Member of Parliament for Wendover, John B. Church, who had served under Lafayette in the American Revolution and married Miss Schuyler of New York. Church's house was quite a political

GOUVERNEUR MORRIS

salon, frequented by Pitt and Burke and Fox; Morris of course visited there. In September, business affairs called him back to Paris, where he stayed until March, 1790.

At Paris Morris witnessed the growing excesses of the French Revolution, came to know the Duke of Orleans (afterwards King Louis Philippe) whom he later met in the United States, and gave good advice to various troubled and highly placed Frenchmen. In March, 1790, he was back in London again, staying in Froome's Hotel.

There now began a remarkable official or semi-official connection of Morris with the British Foreign Office. His Majesty's Government had not yet appointed a Minister to the United States, alleging rather feebly, first, that they were waiting for the Federal Constitution to come into effect, and secondly, that they desired to send a distinguished diplomatist and one agreeable to the American people, but that none wished to go so far.[1] There was no American Minister to the Court of St. James's since the departure of John Adams from London in February, 1788; and the apparent reluctance on the British side to appoint a British Minister at Philadelphia interposed at any rate a moral difficulty in the way of regular negotiation. Morris, therefore, was authorised by President George Washington to negotiate, simply on the authority of the President's letter, with the Duke of Leeds concerning still unexecuted clauses of the peace treaty of 1783. Morris

[1] *The Diary and Letters of Gouverneur Morris*, edited by A. C. Morris (1889), I, 311.

was also authorised to converse with His Majesty's Ministers on the possibility of their entering into a treaty of commerce with the United States.

The chief question at issue was the northwestern posts, Ogdensburg, Oswego, Niagara, Erie, Sandusky, Detroit, and Mackinaw. Great Britain, according to the peace treaty of 1783, was to hand over these to the Americans, but she still held them because (so it was alleged) the Americans were not carrying out their treaty obligations towards the Loyalists; that is, towards colonists who had supported Great Britain in the Revolutionary War. Morris speedily obtained an interview with the Duke of Leeds, Secretary of State, and established excellent personal relations. Regarding the British excuse for not sending a minister to Philadelphia, he tactfully said, 'My Lord, you cannot want men well qualified, and I am certain that there are many who will be glad to accept it.' With regard to the dispute about the northwestern posts, and the British counterclaim that the Americans had not carried out their obligations under the treaty of peace, Morris said: 'that my private opinion had always been that it would be proper for us to execute the treaty fully on our part, and then call for execution by them (the British), for that if each were to delay until the other should act, all treaties would be illusory.' The Duke of Leeds 'agreed in the propriety of this observation.' The question of the northwestern posts was not settled until the Jay Treaty was made in 1794, but Morris has the credit of making a good beginning of the negotiation. 'We do not think it worth while to go to war with you for these posts,' he told Pitt, '*but we know our rights, and will avail ourselves of them when time and circumstances may suit.*' [1]

Morris seems always to have established himself easily and naturally at the centre of political interest. It was intelligible, of course, that he should be well received by Charles James Fox, who, even in the Revolutionary War itself, had been considered to be definitely pro-American. Morris first met Fox at dinner at the house of Mr. Church, the Whig Member of Parliament for Wendover who had fought for the Americans. The company 'sat pretty late after dinner.' Fox scrutinised Morris very closely, to see what sort of man he was, and then talked very freely. The great man's manners were simple, and his conversation frank. He had the smallness of mind, however, to speak lightly of Chatham, and to depreciate his services in the Seven Years' War. He also spoke contemptuously of the Duke of Leeds, and alleged that Lord Hawkesbury and Grenville were indisposed towards the United States, but that Pitt was 'rather friendly than otherwise.' Fox, said Morris, had a mind 'like a clouded sun'; he only required 'temperance, application, and the possession of competence' (*sic*), to make him a very great man. Unfortunately a continuation of his former habits seemed now necessary 'to keep him alive.' Morris heard Fox and also Burke speaking in the long-drawn-out trial of Warren Hastings in the House of Lords. Neither of the two famous orators on this occasion was brilliant: Burke, obviously a genius, but 'vague,

[1] *Diary and Letters of Morris*, I, 330. The italics are Morris's.

loose, desultory, confused'; Fox, 'a slovenly speaker,' though acute and discerning.

The social atmosphere, which John Adams had found a little chilly, was warm and genial for such an agreeable man as Morris. Lord Lansdowne, a great Whig magnate, was 'full of love and kindness for America.' At 'routs' and balls which were magnificently conducted, and attended by the Prince of Wales, the Duke of Orleans (Philippe Egalité) and many grand people, the prevailing manner, in spite of the reserve of the English, was 'very well,' in spite of Morris being an American. Naturally, he went often to the house of his sister-in-law, the Duchess of Gordon. He dined with members of the *corps diplomatique* and found the turtle soup better with them. Nevertheless he was a little bored with his London life. The long games of cards were just 'dull drudgery.' Morris would just look in at the room where the gambling and faro tables were and then go away, 'for the party is to me vastly dull.'

It was much more amusing on the Continent, and he was glad to return to Paris in the autumn of the year 1790. He went to a round of dinners there and saw the political situation going from bad to worse. Many French people wanted him to help them to invest their capital in American land. They expected to be able to raise *châteaux* in parks studded with fine forest trees, and to find superb highways over the pathless deserts. His observations on the course that France was following were very acute; the steady output of paper money was acting as a 'great liquidator of the public debt,' and the nation was working its way 'to a new state of active energy.' He thought that the intervening state of confusion would call forth men of talent. Nevertheless he could also see *guerre, famine, peste,* approaching. Later on he was prophesying the rise of a military despot who would find 'abundant resources in the soil, climate and industry of so fine a country.'[1]

In February, 1792, Morris received his appointment as Minister of the United States to France. He bought a 'neat little house' at Sainport on the bank of the Seine with about twenty acres of land, twenty-seven miles by road from Paris. When Commodore Paul Jones died at Paris on July 18, 1792, Morris was present with him at the last and had to arrange for his funeral. Trouble soon arose between the French and American Governments over the activities of Genêt, the French Minister to the United States, who was issuing privateer licenses. The French Government demanded the recall of Morris, whose appointment, to his inexpressible relief, was terminated on August 1, 1794. He packed up his goods, his 'books, liquors, linens, furniture, plate and carriages,' and had them shipped to New York. Among the 'liquors' was a large quantity of Imperial Tokay, sealed with the arms of Austria, a present from the Empress Maria Theresa to her daughter, Marie Antoinette, Queen of France. Morris had bought this wine during the Reign of Terror at a cheap grocery store for twenty-five cents a bottle. It lasted the Morris family until 1848.

[1] *Diary and Letters,* II, 189, and I, 383.

Before following his possessions to America, Morris decided to travel a little more. He made a leisurely journey through France to Switzerland; visited Necker and Madame de Staël at Coppet on the Lake of Geneva; went by way of Berne and Basle into Germany, to Hamburg, and so by ship to England. He found the scenery, as he sailed up the Thames, 'beautiful beyond description.' This was in June, 1795. He went to his hotel in Covent Garden.

The diplomatic situation in England was now quite good. Jay, who had come and gone, making the treaty that became so unpopular in America, was 'universally liked' in London. Thomas Pinckney, the regular Minister of the United States to the Court of St. James's, was not so well liked, but he had gone off on a visit to Spain for the time being. Morris met at dinner Mr. Burges, head of the American department of the Foreign Office; and through Burges he was introduced to Lord Grenville, the Secretary of State for Foreign Affairs, the intimate friend of the Prime Minister, William Pitt. A warm friendship was formed between Morris and Grenville; in time the American became an important adviser and correspondent of the Secretary of State concerning the·situation on the Continent.

In England these were anxious times. Wheat was selling at one hundred shillings a quarter, and there were bread riots. Grand dinner-parties and 'routs' were, apparently, given up now, although there was a lot of dining and supping in a quiet way. Morris often went to the Piazza Coffee-house, Covent Garden. He celebrated the 4th of July there (1795) with 'a host of

Americans...; but I leave them early, very early.'
On another occasion he saw Boswell, Johnson's biographer, at the Piazza Coffee-house. The Prime Minister, Pitt, dined at six precisely; guests who arrived late
took their seats with dinner already going on. Morris
arrived punctually. Pitt threw off the cares of state
at dinner; 'the wines were good and the conversation
flippant.' The day before Morris dined with him, Pitt's
windows at Number 10 Downing Street had been broken
by the mob, but this did not seem to affect his serenity.

As there was not much business, public or private,
for Morris to do, he went off on a tour through the
south of England. He travelled in his own carriage
with his own servant and found hospitality with a
friend at nearly every stage. The scenery greatly interested him, and so did the soil; he carefully considered
the subject of fertilizers, and the probable return from
an intelligent cultivation of the soil.

At Portsmouth, the Governor, the Admiral and other
naval officers showed him every attention. From there
he went 'over hilly down and heath, on roads that are
as fine as it is possible to imagine them,' to Salisbury.
'As soon as we alight, I go to see the Cathedral, which
is by far the lightest and handsomest Gothic building
I ever saw.' From Salisbury he drove to Exeter, and
from there to Plymouth; near here his brother, the
General, was in camp; Morris met all the high officers.
From Plymouth he went to Bristol, Chepstow, Tintern;
thence to Bath, where he found the *ci-devant* Grand
Vicar of Bordeaux taking a walk in the streets. He
entertained the vicar at dinner on cold fowl, lobster

and salad. The Duke of Beaufort showed him the
pictures, gardens and park of Badminton. From there
he crossed the Cotswolds to Burford where he found an
excellent inn with a dining-room used by the Pilgrims.
The waiter was one of the few really contented men;
he was not rich, but he was happy and healthy; 'Says
he, "what is riches without health?"'

From Burford Morris went through Witney to
Blenheim, to see the Duke of Marlborough's palace; 'it
would be difficult,' he writes of Vanbrugh's master-
piece, 'to cover more space and have less room.... If
ever it should fall to a munificent and hospitable
owner, I do not see where he would put his guests.'
Oxford he found in vacation (August). He noted with
concern that the air was corroding the stone of the
ancient colleges, as it is still doing. From Oxford he
went along the Thames Valley to Maidenhead, branched
off to visit Lord Grenville at Dropmore (but Grenville
was away), and at ten minutes after four on August 17
he arrived at Wimbledon, where he dined that very
evening with Lord Gower and Lady Sutherland.

After staying for a few days with Lord Gower, and
writing a long letter to George Washington on the
situation in Europe, Morris went off on another British
tour. This time he drove north, through East Anglia,
seeing the Great Bed of Ware and visiting Cambridge.
He attended service at King's College Chapel, 'a sort
of chanting' in which it was difficult to distinguish what
was said; 'the Almighty,' commented this son of the
Age of Reason, 'from his quality of omniscience, is of
course apprised of it.' Birmingham, Sheffield, Leeds,

gave him opportunities to study manufactories and wage-rates.

At Edinburgh he was struck with the height of the houses. The gallery of Holyrood Palace, with its alleged portraits of Scottish kings, he considered to be one of the most curious in Europe. He was entertained by the Scottish nobility to good dinners with excellent wines. From Edinburgh he went to Stirling, Perth, Dunkeld, Blair Atholl. The common report of the poverty of Scotland he considered to be a gross exaggeration. 'John Bull seriously believes, and as seriously relates, the wretchedness of his Northern brethren, which I dare say existed at the Union; but the culture of a part of Scotland is equal, if not superior to any in the island.'

Morris spent a day or two with the Duke and Duchess of Atholl, and left Blair Atholl in the Duke's carriage. At Taymouth the rain was so incessant that he accepted Lord Bredalbane's pressing invitation to extend his stay. Lord Bredalbane said that the Duke of Atholl could ride one hundred and ten miles without going off his estates, and this in a straight line. Morris went fishing with Lord Bredalbane on Loch Tay, but found, as others have been known to do, that the fish would take neither fly nor worm. On returning to the house, there were two local clergymen on a visit. There followed some serious conversation on the condition of the people, and then the two clergymen left early; but, as Morris's valet told him afterwards, it was to 'take a dish of tea with the upper servants.'

When Morris reached Inverary, he found the Duke

of Argyle out for the moment. So he returned and
dined at his inn. The Duke came back, however, and
at once sent the American an invitation to dinner. So
Morris went up to the Castle and sat through the
repast, but ate nothing. After dinner the Duke's two
unmarried daughters 'sang a duetto for the old gentleman.' On the morrow, the Duke, who was passionately
interested in agriculture, took him in a chaise round the
grounds, and showed him the work going on. At dinner
they had, 'among other things,' roebuck, which was
very common game in the neighbourhood.

From Inverary Morris drove on to Buchanan, the
seat of the Duke of Montrose, who also entertained him.
They discussed the prevailing growth of manufactures,
or what now would be called the Industrial Revolution;
the Duke considered this to be a doubtful benefit, and
Morris considered that the opinion was worth weighing.
On the way from Buchanan to Glasgow he looked carefully at the Forth and Clyde Canal. 'When I see this,
my mind opens to a view of wealth for the interior of
America which hitherto I had rather conjectured than
seen.' Towards the end of October (1795) Morris
crossed into England and passed through the Lake
District. 'I rode almost round the famous Derwent-
water Lake, which is nothing compared with those in
Scotland, either for size or depth.' Borrowdale seemed
perfectly remote, 'but now the wealth and idleness of
Britain have made it a place of great resort.' After
going by Windermere, Morris visited the Bishop of
Llandaff and Mrs. Watson at their estate, Colgarth
Park. The bishop had a fine estate and was a good

landlord. At dinner there was a dish of the famous Windermere char, which Morris considered no better than a very good trout. He next went to Liverpool, Warwick, Stratford-on-Avon, and on November 23 (1795) was back in his hotel in Covent Garden. It is doubtful whether anyone, at any rate any republican ex-enemy American, can ever have been entertained by so many high noblemen on a single journey. He had gone thirteen hundred miles with his own carriage and horses.

Morris was to be received in a still higher circle than that of the dukes. Two days after coming back to London he went to Court. He was presented to King George, who took him for an Englishman, then recollecting, said, 'You have been a good while in this country.' There followed some conversation with the king on the political situation in France and Holland. King George knew General Morris, of the British army, and remarked on the likeness of the two brothers; as always in social intercourse, he was gentle and kind and amiable. Shortly afterwards Morris went to a City dinner at which George Washington's health was drunk. Morris remained in London through the winter of 1795-96, witnessing debates in Parliament, and meeting statesmen and members of high society continually.

In June, 1796, he departed to the Continent, where he travelled for over two years more, in Switzerland, Germany, and Austria. All the courts received and knew him; if he required an introduction, the British Ambassador would supply it. All this time he was writing long reports on the political situation on the Continent to Lord Grenville, the British Secretary of State for Foreign Affairs. His advice was wise, and his reports contain material of high interest. He retained faith in England throughout the long war. 'The state of your finances,' he wrote, 'is far from encouraging, but yet I am convinced that (unless panic-struck) you will yet get through well.'

In October, 1798, this citizen of the world returned to his native country and never left it during the rest of his life, which was entirely spent in public work. He saw the greatness that was coming: 'the proudest Empire in Europe,' he wrote to his friend, John Parish of London, 'is but a bubble compared to what America *will* be and *must* be, in the course of two centuries, perhaps of one.' The War of 1812 he considered to be simply madness, the work of men, he said, 'who for more than twenty years have lavished on Britain the bitterest vulgarity of Billingsgate because she impressed her seamen for self-defence.' Apparently a confirmed bachelor, he had married long after coming back to America the daughter of an old friend in 1809. He was elected to the Senate, took part in New York public life, and maintained also his correspondence with Europe. He lived to sail up the Hudson on a steamship, and to be President of the New York Historical Society. On November 6, 1816, he died at Morrisania at the age of sixty-four.

Cosmopolitanism did not make Gouverneur Morris cease to be an American. It made Benjamin Thompson, Count Rumford, an American, Englishman, Bavarian, and Frenchman. He was born in 1753 at Woburn,

Massachusetts. He became clerk and assistant in a store at Salem, where he and Samuel Curwen knew each other. At the age of nineteen he married a well-to-do widow and settled down — for a time — on a farm at Rumford (now Concord), New Hampshire. When the Revolutionary War broke out, he offered himself for service in the American army, but was refused. He then sailed for England (leaving his wife whom he never saw again) and obtained an appointment in the British War Office under Lord George Germaine. Before the end of the war, however, he returned to America, where he took command of a regiment of colonial dragoons. He had a brief but creditable period of active service, and then returned to England in 1783. Finding little to do there, he went on travel in the Rhineland, obtained an introduction to the Elector of Bavaria, was taken into service, and rose to be chief Bavarian Minister and a Count of the Holy Roman Empire, taking his title from the farm at Rumford in New Hampshire. In fifteen years of service at Munich, Count Rumford made an abiding mark on Bavarian history, for he was an active and beneficent reformer. His daughter came over from the United States and kept house for him. In 1799 he retired from the Bavarian service and went to live at Paris, where he married the widow of the chemist Lavoisier, and entertained the learned men of the city. The fact that England was at war with France seems not to have interfered with his habits, comforts, or studies at all. He kept a house in London and frequently went there on visits. Wherever he went, he did good, reorganising hospitals, introducing improvements in

cooking, dietetics, sanitation. He was a Fellow of the
Royal Society, and bountifully supported scientific
bodies in England and the United States, and founded
the Royal Institution of London. Count Rumford died
at Paris in 1814.[1]

[1] There is a brilliant chapter on Rumford in L. Einstein, *Divided Loyalties*,
114–50.

V

THE ARTISTS

BY REASON of their profession, artists are among the most travelled of all craftsmen; and in a place congenial to their art they may stay for years, even for a lifetime. At the end of the eighteenth century, and again at the end of the nineteenth, there were American artists of world-wide reputation who made their homes in London. John Singleton Copley, Benjamin West, and John Trumbull were in the earlier period; Edwin Abbey, John S. Sargent, James McNeill Whistler (and others besides these) were in the later period.

Benjamin West was born in 1738 at Springfield near Swarthmore in Pennsylvania. His father, John West, was a Quaker of Long Crendon, Buckinghamshire, who had migrated to America in the reign of Charles II. The young West was brought up in circumstances favourable to artistry. 'The benevolent fraternity of Quakers had that simplicity of manners and that serenity of look which artists love, while around them the nations of Europe had scattered their children as thick as the trees of the forest. The gay Frenchman, the

plodding Dutchman, the energetic Englishman, the
laborious Scot — all were there, each emblazoned with
the peculiarities, and speaking the language, of his
native soil.' [1]

The lithe and graceful Indians, peaceful and friendly
in Pennsylvania, furnished West with living models of
the naked figure. Cherokee Indians are said to have
given him his first lessons in colour-mixing, as well as in
archery. His school education was rather casual; West
has come down in history as the only President of the
Royal Academy who found a difficulty in spelling. His
youthful years, however, were full of artistic suggestion;
peaceful Quaker as he was, he loved to hear of the characters and deeds of the Greeks and Romans. He listened with the liveliest interest to tales which his brother brought back from service in General Forbes's
great march from Philadelphia to Fort Duquesne in
1758. There was one particularly strange tale of the
finding by his son of the skeleton of Major Sir Peter
Halket, who had been killed in the forest fighting under
General Braddock in 1756. The imagination of the
young West was kindled to a flame which later showed
itself in the picture of 'The Death of Wolfe.'

There was some scope for a portrait-painter who
charged low fees at Philadelphia. West set up his easel
there at the age of eighteen. Soon he moved to New
York, where he could ask higher prices. There he saw
and copied a Saint Ignatius of Murillo, captured from a
Spanish ship. Like all artists he felt that he must see

[1] Cunningham, *The Lives of the Most Eminent British Painters* (ed. 1879),
I, 284.

Italy, and soon rather than late. So he took advantage of the sailing of a flour-ship to Italy, where the harvest had failed, and of a present of fifty pounds from a New York merchant interested in his art, to go to Leghorn. From there he went on by carriage to Rome, entering the Eternal City on July 10, 1760. America never saw him again. He was twenty-two years old, and was able partly to maintain himself by painting portraits for the English colony in Rome. The rest of his maintenance he obtained from gifts from Governor Hamilton and other patrons in Pennsylvania. He was the first native American who went to study the fine arts in Europe, and Americans at home felt proud of him. After three fruitful years of work in Rome and other places of Italy, he set out for London, arriving there on June 20, 1763.

West only meant to visit London and the home counties, and then to return to America. Englishmen and Scotsmen whom he had known in Rome now welcomed him in their houses and clubs. He made journeys to Hampton Court, Windsor, Blenheim, Reading (where a half-brother lived), and to Bath, the Vanity Fair of English society. Then he took chambers in Covent Garden, in the heart of literary, dramatic, and artistic London. There was an opening for a painter of historical subjects: Reynolds only did portraits, Hogarth was old, Gainsborough was considered chiefly as a landscape-painter. 'The prudent American saw that he had a fair field and no opponents.' [1] He decided to stay and make his career in England. When they heard this, the generous British artists came round to his

[1] Cunningham, *op. cit.*, I, 302.

chambers and applauded his decision. He was now one of them. The rest of his long tranquil life was passed in England. The young woman to whom he had been engaged in America came over, after five years of separation, and they were married at St. Martin's-in-the-Fields. This was in 1765, the year of the passage into law of the Stamp Act.

The 'Pensilvanian,' as Horace Walpole called him, had numerous and very distinguished friends. There was Edmund Burke, in whom West was conscious of something mysterious until suddenly it flashed upon the American that he was 'the brother of the chief of the Benedictine Monks at Parma.' Burke's family connections are somewhat uncertain, but it is not at all likely that the Irish monk of Parma had any connection with him. Another friend of West was Dr. Johnson, in spite of the doctor's vigorous declaration to Boswell: 'I am willing to love all mankind except an American.'

Dr. Drummond, Archbishop of York, introduced West to George III. The record of this interview, like that of all George's private affairs, puts the king in a kind and honest light. West, on the suggestion of Archbishop Drummond, was painting a picture of Agrippina bringing back the ashes of Germanicus, as described by Tacitus. Dr. Drummond brought the young painter to St. James's Palace.

> The King received West with easy frankness, assisted him to place the Agrippina in a favourable light, removed the attendants, and brought in the Queen, to whom he presented our Quaker. He related to her Majesty the

history of the picture, and bade her notice the simplicity of the design and the beauty of the colouring. 'There is another noble Roman subject,' observed his Majesty, 'the departure of Regulus from Rome — would it not make a fine picture?' 'It is a magnificent subject,' said the painter. 'Then,' said the King, 'You shall paint it for me.' He turned with a smile to the Queen and said, 'The Archbishop made one of his sons read Tacitus to Mr. West, and I would have read Livy to him myself — but that part of the history which describes the departure of Regulus is unfortunately lost.' He then repeated his command that the picture should be painted.

Artists are seldom much interested in politics. West did not allow the controversies over the Stamp Act nor the Revolutionary War itself to spoil his peace of mind or interrupt his work. This work was sufficiently important. West is a veritable landmark in the history of British art. He had considerable vogue. George III greatly favoured him, made him historical painter to the crown, and surveyor of the royal pictures, and gave him a pension of a thousand pounds a year. West was good-natured and by no means unbusinesslike. In the classical pictures which he painted for the king, he introduced the features of the royal family in the heroes of Greece and Rome. It was not all this, however, that made West a landmark in the history of British painting. It was when he decided to paint 'The Death of Wolfe' in the military costumes of the year 1759, and not in the panoply of the Greeks and Romans, that something new came into British art.

This quiet Quaker had a better idea of what a battle-field looked like than had Sir Joshua Reynolds, who tried hard to dissuade him from what was considered to be a daring and unjustifiable innovation. 'The Death of Wolfe,' as engraved by Woollett, is one of the best known of modern pictures. The excitement of battle is in it, the nobility of sacrifice, the solemnity of death. 'The Indian warrior, watching the dying hero to see if he equalled in fortitude the children of the deserts, is a fine stroke of nature and poetry.' To the Englishmen of the eighteenth century and the Englishmen of today the picture is the living, the essential rendering of the Age of Chatham; and probably nobody but an American could have painted it. Sir Joshua Reynolds, although he had been against West's design, after sitting for half-an-hour in front of the finished work, rose and said: 'West has conquered; he has treated his subject as it ought to be treated; I retract my objections. I foresee that this picture will not only become one of the most popular, but will occasion a revolution in art.' Nelson told West that he could 'never pass a print-shop where "The Death of Wolfe" was in the window, without stopping to look at it; and he asked the artist why he had not painted more pictures like it. "Because there are no more subjects," said West. "Damn it," said the simple hero, "I didn't think of that." West suggested that Nelson's intrepidity might provide another such scene. "Then I hope that I shall die in the next battle," said Nelson. He sailed a few days afterwards, and the result was on the canvas before us.'[1]

[1] George Ticknor, *Journal*, June 23, 1815; *Life of George Ticknor* (1876), I, 63.

From this moment, it might be said, Reynolds and West divided between them the most lucrative of artists' practice in the England of George III. Sir Joshua had, as Allan Cunningham points out, almost a monopoly of painting the dignitaries of Church and State outside the palace gates, while West was supreme inside. He painted portraits of members of the royal family, at two thousand guineas each; and decorated St. George's Chapel, Windsor, at fees amounting, apparently, to about £20,000. On the death of Sir Joshua in 1792, West was elected President of the Royal Academy, with the warm approval of George III. The sculptor, Chantrey, executed his bust, now in the National Portrait Gallery of London; and West, always interested in young artists, obtained for Chantrey the commission to make a statue of George Washington for Boston.

Down to his death in 1820, in the same year as his blind master and patron George III died, West was painting historical and scriptural pictures. He had a fine house at 14, Newman Street, a roomy, almost stately mansion, which the dignified, gentle, handsome artist furnished as a gallery of his own pictures, and where he dispensed hospitality to men of art and letters. Benjamin Silliman of Yale, who was travelling in England in 1805, met West and was very kindly received. West had by no means lost his interest in America, and in spite of forty years' absence, still cherished the hope of revisiting his native land. George III, who was a great gentleman, had never, not even during the American War, expected West to conceal sympathy with the Americans. Silliman tells a story that was current in London. During the American War, a nobleman, who was very envious of West's friendship with the king, came into the room in Windsor Castle where the artist was painting while the king was looking on. This was when Lord Cornwallis's victory at Camden had brought a glint of light into the depressing fortunes of the British.

'Mr. West, have you heard the news from town this morning?' asked the Tory nobleman.

'No, sir, I have not seen the papers of today.'

'Then, sir, let me inform you that His Majesty's troops in South Carolina have gained a splendid victory over the rebels, your countrymen. This, I suppose, cannot be very pleasant news to you, Mr. West.'

West, though he saw the snare laid for him, calmly replied: 'No, sir, this is not pleasant news to me, for I can never rejoice at the misfortunes of my countrymen.'

George III, who, hitherto, had taken no notice of the conversation, now said to West: 'Sir, that answer does you honour'; then, turning to the nobleman, he said severely: 'Sir, let me tell *you*, that in my opinion, any man who is capable of rejoicing in the calamities of his country can never make a good subject of any government.'[1] Silliman saw George III in 1805 at Drury Lane Theatre, and wrote that he was 'a noble-looking old man' with such a fresh-coloured face, that 'on the whole I think he appears younger than almost any man of his age whom I have ever seen.'

West is buried in St. Paul's Cathedral, beside his

[1] Benjamin Silliman, *Journal of Travels in England, Holland and Scotland* (1812), 161.

great peer, Reynolds. There was a better painter than West among the many young men whom he helped to bring forward. John Singleton Copley was born in 1737, a year before West, at Boston, where he attended the Latin school and gained an excellent knowledge of English literature. He became a very successful portrait-painter at Boston; George Washington was one of his sitters. He married, had a fine family of children, one of whom became Lord Chancellor of England and a peer of the realm with the title of Lord Lyndhurst. He bought a house in Boston, on the Common, and was making an income of three hundred guineas a year, as much, he said, as the poverty of Boston could afford. In fact he had everything to make him happy, except the experience of Europe. When the troubles between the colonies and England became acute, Copley felt that he must go at once or lose his chance perhaps for ever; so in 1774, which was the year before war actually broke out, he risked life and fortune and went off to Europe leaving wife and family behind him. He certainly lost a fortune — the house and land which he owned in Boston; but in the galleries of Italy, especially by studying their sculptures, he perfected his powers of draughtsmanship and became a great artist.

Copley was still in Italy when the American Revolutionary War broke out (April, 1775). His wife and children left Boston and took ship to England, arriving there on June 28, 1775; therefore knowing that his family was safe, Copley quietly went on and finished his travels, taking Austria, Germany, and Holland

on his way to England. He reached London at the end
of 1776.

For some years previously, Copley had been in correspondence with Benjamin West who now helped him
to find sitters in London. He soon had a fine practice
as a portrait-painter, and in 1777 became, with the
support of West, an Associate of the Royal Academy.
He conceived the idea of painting the last appearance
of Chatham in the House of Lords, where the great
statesman fell down in a fit, when answering a question
of the Duke of Richmond. The conception of this
picture was undoubtedly suggested to him by West's
'Death of Wolfe.' Copley made minute studies and
enquiries, and produced the grand scene with all the
actors perfectly portrayed, the dying statesman, the
peers all starting to their feet, except one, the Earl
of Mansfield, who sat still. This picture, which is in
the National Gallery, London, naturally appealed to
Americans (Chatham was speaking on the American
question) as much as to Englishmen. From that moment, Copley was recognised by Boston as one of her
greatest sons.

Historical pictures of this time had in England a
certain vogue which they have never enjoyed to the
same extent since. The invasion of Jersey by the
French towards the end of the American War provided
a theme for a magnificent picture by Copley, now in
the National Gallery, London. The episode depicted
is the stand made by Major Peirson and a handful of
troops, and the death of the young commander. The
Duke of Wellington is said to have called the picture

'the best battle piece he had ever seen.' Copley jour-
neyed to Jersey to make studies for the picture, and
thus was able to paint in the background an 'exact
view of the town of St. Helier's, where the battle was
fought.' Copley's picture of the repulse and defeat
of the Spanish floating batteries at Gibraltar in 1780
is another striking battle piece. 'The scene of desolation
is certainly grand.' [1] It is now in the Guildhall, London.
The vogue of historical pictures was, however, short-
lived; and Copley was fortunate in having portrait-
painting for his regular practice. In this he was ac-
commodating and businesslike, as is proved by the
story of the patron who in a family group insisted on
having his three wives (naturally, only one was living)
painted on the same canvas. When the living wife
insisted on the removal of the other two, Copley
obligingly painted them out. Finally, he had to bring
an action at law before he could obtain payment for
his work on the obliterated portraits.

Copley became a full member of the Royal Academy
in 1783. He continued to paint and exhibit down to
his last years. His home was in George Street, Hanover
Square, where he died on September 9, 1815, at the
age of seventy-eight. Like West, he never returned
to his native land. In his house he had frequent
company. He was a fine old gentleman, fond of splendid
dress and the outward show of magnificence. He was a
great reader of the English classics, his favourite book
being *Paradise Lost*.

The Revolutionary and post-Revolutionary years are

[1] Cunningham, *op. cit.*, II, 236.

the classic period of American painters in England, particularly painters of historical subjects. With West and Copley the name of Trumbull is associated. Trumbull received a good education in Latin and Greek, went to Harvard, and on one occasion met Copley who was still living at Boston in his house on the Common (1772). When the Revolutionary War broke out, Trumbull joined the Continental forces, saw some active service, was made aide-de-camp to George Washington and later deputy adjutant-general in the army of General Gates. He resigned his post in 1776, owing to a controversy with Governor John Hancock, and went to Boston, sick and tired, to carry on the pursuit which he really loved, painting.

In 1779, before the war was over, he applied through an English friend to Lord George Germaine, for permission to go to London to study painting under Benjamin West. Lord George, who as Secretary of State, had responsibility for the conduct of this singular war, answered to the effect: 'that if I chose to visit London for the purpose of studying the fine arts, no notice would be taken by the Government of my past life; but that I must remember that the eye of precaution would be constantly upon me, and I must therefore avoid the smallest indiscretion — but that so long as I avoided all political intervention, and pursued the study of the arts with assiduity, I might rely upon being unmolested.' So in the midst of what was now a great European war, Trumbull took ship, first to France (America's ally against Great Britain), and after an interesting sojourn there, to England. Benjamin Franklin, who was representing the States in Paris, had given him a letter of introduction to West in London. Such were the ways of the patriots and citizens of the world in the Age of Reason.

Trumbull took lodgings in London in the Adelphi. He found plenty of company among American Loyalists from Boston and from other places. In 1780, returning to his lodgings after taking tea with Mr. and Mrs. Channing of Georgia, he was arrested on a charge of high treason, as a reprisal for the execution of Major André, whom Washington had executed as a spy. There was very little choice of prisons, as the London mob had burned them in the anti-Roman Catholic riots of 1780.. The magistrate before whom Trumbull appeared offered him a choice between the Tower of London and Tothill Fields Bridewell. Trumbull chose Tothill Fields because it was quiet, and because the keeper of the Bridewell, who had been butler to the Duke of Northumberland, had the manners of a gentleman. The prison had a pretty little garden. Trumbull did not live in the cells. He hired a room in the keeper's house for a guinea a week. It was neatly furnished and had a handsome *bureau* bed. He could order and pay for whatever he wanted from a neighbouring tap-house. A turnkey brushed his hat, clothes, and shoes in return for the prisoner's allowance of a pennyworth of bread and a penny a day, which Trumbull handed over to him. The gentlemanly keeper knocked at his door and looked in, night and morning, to see that he was safe and to wish him good night and good morning. Benjamin West, who made no secret of his love for

America, interceded for him; but he had to stay in
prison for eight months, copying West's copy of Cor-
reggio's 'Jerome of Parma,' and receiving visits from
Charles James Fox and Edmund Burke. The Trumbull
copy was later deposited in the Gallery at New Haven.
He was finally liberated from prison, West and Copley
becoming sureties for him. After visiting Holland,
Trumbull took ship from Amsterdam to Boston; thence
he went to Lebanon and presented himself to General
Washington; but peace was now being negotiated. He
tried to go on with his art, until his patient but not
very sympathetic father reminded him that Connecticut
was not Athens. Struck with this truth, Trumbull
took ship again, in December, 1783, for London.

On this, his second visit to London, Trumbull had
the best of society: Burke, Benjamin West, in whose
studio he painted daily, Sir Joshua Reynolds, and Sir
Thomas Lawrence whom he came to know as a fellow
student, at the Academy. He began to build up a
practice, painting the portraits of American friends
who came over to London on visits; but battle pieces,
La Hogue, Bunker Hill, Saratoga, found his chief
occupation, along with classical pictures, scenes from
the *Odyssey* or *Iliad* which he had read in boyhood.
The British artists, the great Sir Joshua himself, when
they came to dine with West, would look critically at
Trumbull's pictures of their country's recent defeats
and become enthusiastic over their colouring; the
political aspect of the pictures never occurred to them.

So the time passed on in fruitful work, varied by a
visit to Paris on the invitation of Jefferson, who, while

Minister to France, had come to London in 1785 and interested himself in Trumbull's art. Trumbull stayed in Jefferson's house, at the Grille de Chaillot, and studied the best French masters. He also became intimate with the English miniature-painter, Cosway, who had come over to paint the Duchess of Orleans and her children. In 1786 he was back in London, benefiting from the patronage of another American, the former Revolutionary officer, John Carter, who now, under the name of John Barker Church (apparently his real name), was living in England in great elegance, a Member of Parliament. Trumbull 'frequently dined at his table with distinguished men, such as Sheridan, etc.'

In 1786 Trumbull went over to France again, visiting Jefferson and studying buildings and pictures. In Paris and Versailles, three years before the Revolution, he saw the still magnificent splendour of the *ancien régime*. It was Lent; the opulent clergy, who were hospitable to him, dined magnificently, though without meat. A journey down the Rhine ended the trip. In November he was back in England, and settled down to his great series of pictures of the Revolutionary War. 'The Surrender of Lord Cornwallis' gave him great trouble, because he had to be correct in all the military details, and to paint accurately the portraits of the principal officers of the 'three proud nations' — French, English, and American. His English friends and patrons, with the curious objectivity of the race, were intensely interested in the picture, although some 'extra-patriotic people' disliked his work. The subject of Trumbull's picture of the British triumph at Gibraltar was suggested to him by an Italian friend. He paid two more visits to Paris in 1787 and 1789, witnessing the outbreak of the Revolution and the fall of the Bastille. Then came three years in New York, where he painted Washington's portrait, until 1794 when he returned to England as secretary to John Jay, on a special diplomatic mission. His practice in America had not been very profitable.

The Jay Mission had the practical object of preventing war between Great Britain and the United States, on account of the irritation caused by questions of freedom of the sea during the French Revolutionary War, and by questions left over from the peace treaty of 1783. The Mission not only had a sensible object, but was sensibly carried out. Lord Grenville, as the British Secretary of State, and Mr. Jay had direct and non-committal conversations with each other; 'and the secretaries, Sir James Bland Burges and myself [Trumbull], had a real holiday for a month.' When the two chiefs had agreed on the various disputed points with each other, the secretaries were put to work, 'and had ample occupation.' The treaty was signed at London on November 19, 1794.

This period of diplomatic service was followed by a tour in France and Germany and a speculation in French brandy which the war had run up to famine prices. The speculation failed, luckily without loss of money to Trumbull. He was glad, however, to find occupation and some income in an appointment from the United States Government to act as agent for the execution of the Jay Treaty in London. The duties were varied by another visit to France in 1797, on artist's business, when he met Talleyrand, Lucien Bonaparte, Madame de Staël. Life in France was dangerous then, owing to highway robbers and banditti. Trumbull had an exciting time, and on returning to London forswore dangerous adventures for ever, and betook himself to 'the sober duties' of his Government diplomatic commission, which lasted until 1804.

In this year he sailed to New York and went into practice as a portrait-painter. On July 4, he dined in company with Alexander Hamilton and Aaron Burr and remarked on their odd manner to each other. A few days later occurred the fatal Hamilton-Burr duel. The embargo placed by President Jefferson on foreign commerce in 1808 destroyed the prosperity of Trumbull's merchant patrons; so off he went to England, sailing on December 15, 1808, to resume his practice in London. 'This was almost the last ship that was permitted to sail under this self-denying ordinance — the embargo.' In spite of the 'manifest inclination,' as Trumbull calls it, of President Jefferson towards France, the English gentry ordered pictures from the American artist, and he soon built up a fairly good practice again. His expenses, however, were heavy, and in 1812 he had arranged to return to the United States, when the War of 1812 broke out and stopped him.

The restoration of peace gave Trumbull the opportunity of returning, and returning for good, to America, in 1815. He rented a house on Broadway at twelve hundred dollars a year, and recommenced his practice as a painter. A commission to decorate the dome of the Capitol in Washington confirmed his popularity; the rest of his long busy life was passed in the United States. He died at New York on November 10, 1843.[1]

[1] The passages quoted above are from the *Autobiography of John Trumbull* (New York, 1841).

VI

THE AMERICANS AND EDINBURGH

ASSOCIATION — commercial, social, educational — between Great Britain and America existed, naturally, from the very beginning of the colonial period. In education, the connection was particularly close. The colonial gentry often sent their sons, sometimes their daughters, to Great Britain, for the most part to England, for schooling. The movement in the other direction, from Great Britain to America, was for commerce and emigration only. It is only in very recent years, practically since the World War, that young British men and women have begun to go in considerable numbers to the United States for the purpose of education.

In the colonial period, one of the things of which the Americans most felt the want was medical education. There was no medical school in the American colonies until 1769. Young Americans who aspired to be physicians came for training to Great Britain, and especially to the famous medical school at Edinburgh. In the years 1760–65 some five or six young

Philadelphians came over to Edinburgh and took the medical course: Morgan, Benjamin Rush, 'the Sydenham of America,' father of the statesman Richard Rush, Shippen and others. This brilliant Philadelphian group may almost be considered the founders of the American medical faculty. When they returned home they started the great hospitals of Philadelphia and New York.

The distinguished statesman and diplomatist, Gouverneur Morris, had almost a royal time in Edinburgh during his northern tour of 1795. He took a room in a hotel on the slope of the hill, just north of the High Street. The Scottish aristocracy was very much to the fore. 'Lord Somerville calls.... Sir William Forbes calls.' 'Lord Adam Gordon expresses a wish to see me.' 'Dine with Lord Somerville, who gives me a good dinner with excellent wines. We are three. Sir Richard Ainslie is the third.' 'Dine with Lord Adam Gordon, who is very polite and extremely attentive to me. Lords Somerville and Napier, with General Campbell and others, are of our party. A very good dinner and a pleasant evening.' Such were the main incidents of Morris's visit to Edinburgh. A distinguished Governor of Bengal, Sir John McPherson, told him how he (Sir John) had invented a system of paper money, in order to fill the empty treasury of the East India Company in India and to pay the company's soldiers and servants. The notes were numbered, and were redeemed in numerical order. 'All payments were made in that paper, and the accounts of its redemption regularly published.' Sir John asserted that the French

Revolutionary *assignats* were copied from his currency notes. Morris, who had lived in Paris in the time of the Revolution and *assignats*, did not contradict. 'But I know more of *assignats* than he does,' he privately commented.

Opposite Morris's lodging was the back view of the High Street houses, ten storeys high, where the hill falls away; on the front they were six or seven storeys. Edinburgh had a foreign look. 'If it were not for the signs, etc., in English, one might take it for a French town.' He was amazed by the sight of the New Haven 'fishwives' walking up from Leith with their 'creels' or baskets of fish on their backs, fastened by a strap which went round the forehead (this once familiar sight has now disappeared). Morris was much impressed by seeing the stains at Holyrood Palace of the blood of David Rizzio, Queen Mary's secretary, whom the rough Scottish lords murdered in 1566. Those stains were still visible thirty years ago.

In the early nineteenth century the great attraction to Americans in Great Britain was London, the most vivid and characteristic centre of England's history, society, literature. Oxford was only beginning to draw Americans to it; the vogue of Cambridge came still later. Stratford was coming into appreciation through Washington Irving. The appeal of Edinburgh was particularly strong. 'The society here is certainly excellent,' wrote George Ticknor of Harvard in 1819. 'In open-heartedness I imagine it is almost unrivalled; and what that virtue is, how completely it will cover a multitude of deficiencies, one who has been a stranger and obliged to make strangers his friends, can alone know. It is a great thing, too, to have so much influence granted to talent as there is in Edinburgh, for it breaks down the artificial distinctions of society.'[1]

The northern capital was then at the height of its fame, and rejoiced in an unchallenged intellectual eminence. The *Edinburgh Review* was actually edited, printed, and published in Edinburgh. Scott was embarked on the grand literary progress which was to make him the *doyen* of British letters. The city was studded with clubs — not palatial material structures, but groups of congenial men meeting in a tavern, where wit and wisdom came forth as sparkling as in the Paris *salons*. A brilliant and fashionable society, aristocracy of birth and of intellect, rivalled even the metropolis of London. The University of Edinburgh, shaped by men of European reputation, was something far greater than even a great national institution; young Englishmen destined for high politics — the young Palmerston, Lord John Russell — came there for learning and experience.

Alexander Carlyle has described the society of Edinburgh, at a rather earlier period, in his autobiography. One of the first numbers of the *North American Review* described it in the early nineteenth century. Many of the American readers of the *Review* would recognise the picture from their own experience. The writer, who was an American correspondent of the year 1814,[2] had found in his travels much stiffness in certain places,

[1] *Life of George Ticknor* (1876), I, 277.
[2] *North American Review*, I, 183 ff.

and had heard of eighteenth-century pompousness and formality as still persisting at the courts of St. James's, Vienna, Dresden. He had formed theories about the improvement of society: 'from this tyranny of un-meaning forms we were delivered by the superior re-finement of the French. Under the influence of *petits soupers*, a style of society admitting of much nature, wit and at the same time elegance, was established.' He held, too, 'that refinement of society has in all ages kept an equal pace with the progress of women, and that it has moreover commenced everywhere among literary men.' He found all these things, something of French elegance, progress of women, literary men held in honour, in the social life of Edinburgh. The New Town was 'the winter residence of a greater part of the rich families in Scotland'; and along with them were all the accessories of accomplishment and refinement. He describes Edinburgh:

> The seat of a University, to which 1800 or 2000 students annually resort, many of them young noblemen and men of fortune, who add something to the gaiety and little to the industry of the place. This is also the portico, in which several of the most distinguished literary men in Great Britain assemble their disciples. There are moreover an-nually produced here several bulky poems, besides numer-ous small effusions, various histories, learned treatises, lots of books of travels, scores of new plays, abun-dance of journals, reviews, a few novels, editions of black letter and encyclopædias, besides registers, almanacks, catechisms.

Clearly, intellectual life in Edinburgh was very active, its output certainly comparable with that of

London. Also the intellectual life was fashionable. The American correspondent of 1814 continues:

> The society is then reckoned very literary. It is no pedantry to talk about books. Lord Byron's monthly muse makes conversation for the next month's routes [*sic*]. The young men walk up and down the street with an elegant book under their arm instead of a small stick. The character of the place betrays itself in various other symptoms; and while the fashion of some towns is the most approved arrangement of a dinner-party, the prevailing fashion of Edinburgh is for literature. Not that this makes them ceremonious, or takes away a relish for the thousand brilliant trifles and elegancies of life.

Nature, in this American's view, had given to the Scots a country 'hardly able to raise the common means of subsistence'; and their heads, like the country, were 'tough, inflexible, indefatigable.' The Scots of the higher classes, however, were 'among the most hospitable in the world.' They were 'enlightened, well-educated'; 'It is very seldom that the part of the world from which one may happen to come ever creates a look of surprise or a cool reception. Nationality in the senate may be the highest virtue; but in the drawing-room it is the lowest prejudice.'

The *rout*, or evening 'at home,' was the universal form of entertainment in high society during the two months' winter season which the Scottish nobility spared for Edinburgh from their castles or their travels. In these *routs*, which began about nine in the evening and ended before midnight, university professors, men of letters, Lowland lairds and Highland chieftains, and the judges and learned lawyers mingled together without formality, proving that learning could exist outside convents and colleges, and that elegance could be found outside the courts of the great. Wit banished the *ennui* of wealth, banished also tedious and fruitless political bickering; the 'frequent presence of literary men' ensured this.

Our American was fortunate to see at his *routs*, Mr. Playfair, man of fashion, science, and letters, called the d'Alembert of Edinburgh; Sir Walter Scott, the man most 'in demand' at all functions; Sir Archibald Alison, the historian; and Mrs. Grant of Laggan, famous for her familiar writings both in Britain and North America, and herself a 'stronghold' of conversation, although it was said that she had only three subjects for her vivacious and bountiful talk — the adventures of Mrs. Grant of Laggan, the beautiful lochs and vales of the Highlands, and the greatness of the British nation. She was, as a matter of fact, a really nice old lady. Ticknor said that an American found himself more easily at home in her drawing-room than anywhere else in Edinburgh. Mrs. Grant knew many Americans and liked them. She wrote to an American friend: 'The American character has been much raised among our literary people here, by a constellation of persons of brilliant talents and polished manners by whom we were delighted and dazzled last winter. A Mr. Preston of Virginia, and his friend from Carolina, whose name I cannot spell for it is French [Hugh S. Legaré], Mr. Ticknor and Mr. Cogswell were the most distinguished representatives of your new world. A handsome and high-bred Mr. Ralston, from

Philadelphia, whose mind seemed equal to his other attractions, left also a very favourable impression of Transatlantic accomplishments. These were all very agreeable persons, Mr. Ticknor pre-eminently so, and I can assure you ample justice was done to their merits here.'

The Americans were drawn to Edinburgh by many things: by the fame of the University, by the charm of the literary society, by the unique situation, unsurpassed in grandeur and beauty. Also, the Revolutionary War was regarded as an English War; the Scots escaped the prejudice, the rankling bitterness, left by the war in the minds of Americans against Englishmen. Particularly, if George Ticknor's view is correct, the Americans were drawn by the 'open-heartedness' of the Scot, they found his character expansive. McLellan quotes from Ticknor: 'In open-heartedness I imagine it is almost unrivalled.'

The number of American students at the University of Edinburgh in the early decades of the nineteenth century was apparently generally about twenty-five or thirty. Even the great European War did not keep them away. Benjamin Silliman, who spent a winter in Edinburgh in 1805–06, found twenty-five Americans, mostly from New England, at the University. Edinburgh was congenial to them. Silliman noted that the manners of the citizens were very similar to those of New England. Even a characteristic Scottish dish like porridge had its counterpart, the hasty pudding of New England. Silliman was impressed with the high fame of the University with its fourteen hundred students and twenty-five professors, all, or almost all, men of renown. Another American, Henry B. McLellan, who came to Scotland a little later, admired the professors but found the conduct of the students not all that could be desired. The celebrated 'Christopher North' (Professor Wilson), whose *Noctes Ambrosianae* charmed the British and American public and depicted Edinburgh literary and social life at its best, poured forth his wit and eloquence before scarcely appreciative classes. Wilson, as N. P. Willis of Philadelphia observed on a visit in 1833, had a wide knowledge of American poetry. McLellan went to hear the professor lecture and noted in his journal: [1]

> Attended classes. Heard a fine burst of eloquence from Professor Wilson against the impropriety of the loud whispering of the students in the lecture-room. The conduct of some of these young men is frequently very unbecoming the refinement of scholars and gentlemen. Often have I seen them with an air of flippant disrespect to the courtesies of company and to the claims of scholarship, remain with their hats on during a whole lecture, with an assurance unbecoming the aspirant for the honours of a university. This though much palliated by, is much to be ascribed to, the faults of the system.

Professor Wilson, and also Dr. Chalmers, the most celebrated Scottish divine of the nineteenth century, treated Mr. McLellan 'rather like a son than a stranger from a strange land.' This was in 1832, just after the publication of Mrs. Trollope's inopportune book with the offensive title, *The Domestic Manners of the Americans*. This book was naturally a subject of conversa-

[1] H. B. McLellan, *Journal of a Residence in Scotland* (1834), 204.

tion at the breakfast-parties and supper-parties of
Edinburgh. When at 'Mr. H——'s breakfast,' a
young gentleman spoke in favourable terms of the
work, Mr. McLellan with good sense replied simply:
'that I had read a part of the book, and regretted its
publication, more for the injury it might do the English
than ourselves. For what can Americans think of a
country where such a work passes for sterling?' Mr.
McLellan observed in his journal that Europeans in
general and the Scots 'in particular' were very ignorant about America. This criticism seems to have been
justified, for Dr. Chalmers, who was to be the great
leader and founder of the Free Church, remarked to
McLellan (a student of divinity of a free New England
church) that he 'could not conceive how a country can
do without an established church.'

Mr. McLellan did not restrict his knowledge of Scotland to Edinburgh. He went into Fife, Stirlingshire,
saw the Trossachs, visited Glasgow and had a favourable impression of the university there. The city,
though it contained fine public and private buildings,
fell short of Edinburgh (so he thought) except in the
university buildings. Glasgow University was very
large, ancient, with two inner courtyards connected by
arches and gates. The courts were thronged with students in 'fantastical red gowns.' Connected with the
University, there was the Hunterian Museum, an
admirable scientific institution, with a gallery of paintings that gave our American 'exquisite delight.'

This talented and amiable young man, a graduate of
Harvard and a student of the Andover Theological

Seminary in Massachusetts, was only twenty-one years old when he visited Scotland, and wrote his sensible, observant journal. He returned to Boston in 1832 and died shortly afterwards of typhus. He had determined to write a work on Great Britain, for which he brought back voluminous materials, and had made some progress with it, when his labours were arrested by death. It was just after this that another philosophic American, the greatest of his kind, paid a visit to Edinburgh. This was Emerson, who during his first journey to Great Britain in 1833, preached in the Unitarian Church in Young Street, Edinburgh, on August 18. Alexander Ireland, who was later one of his biographers, was among the congregation.

The late eighteenth century and the early nineteenth century were admittedly the heyday of Scottish metropolitan life. After this, Edinburgh, while remaining a city of great distinction, would not claim to rival London; Athens could not prevail against Rome; nor could Weimar keep all its distinguished men of letters, artists, scholars, men of affairs, in face of the absorbing interests of Berlin. Nevertheless, Edinburgh remains a capital of rare beauty, and of vivid social and cultural interests; its university is one of the great schools of Europe. When Charles W. Eliot, President of Harvard University, paid a long visit to Great Britain in 1879, in order to investigate conditions of academic institutions, he naturally went, among other places, to Edinburgh, where he had a good friend in the Principal, Sir Alexander Grant. Eliot wrote: 'Edinburgh was fine.... The Scotch are full of humor.... I had great fun lunching and dining with a number of University men. They were uproarious and amusing "to a degree," so I laughed till I cried.' Mr. Eliot was a man not easily moved. His biographer wonders what those Scottish jests could have been. Mr. Eliot's colleagues at Harvard 'would gladly have known.' [1]

[1] H. James, *Charles W. Eliot* (1930), I, 332.

❖◆❖◆❖◆❖◆❖◆❖◆❖

VII

THE ENGLAND OF
WASHINGTON IRVING

Towards the end of the French War there was the Anglo-American War of 1812-14, which neither side wanted to fight and neither side knew how to stop. The War of 1812 literally 'petered out' when each side had burnt the other's capital [1] and there was nothing more to do. An inconclusive peace (which the men of *Realpolitik* say is always worse than none) ended the war; and this inconclusive peace at once assumed a curiously stable and satisfactory aspect, and has endured ever since. Englishmen, as their way is, seized the moment of the close of hostilities to resume their mobile habits, and the long stream of Halls, Murrays, Mrs. Trollopes, and Marryats began.

The American, on his side, might have been thought likely to remain for a time content with seeing his own country first. Washington Irving, in 1818, faced this idea boldly.

[1] York, Ontario, burned on April 27, 1813; Washington, D.C., on August 24, 1814.

Had I been merely influenced by a love of fine scenery, I should have felt little desire to seek elsewhere its gratifications; for on no country have the charms of nature been more prodigally lavished. Her mighty lakes, like oceans of liquid silver; her mountains, with their bright aerial tints; her valleys, teeming with wild fertility; her tremendous cataracts, thundering in their solitudes; her boundless plains, waving with spontaneous verdure; her broad deep rivers, rolling in solemn silence to the ocean; her trackless forests, where vegetation puts forth all its magnificence; her skies, kindling with the magic of summer clouds and glorious sunshine: — no, never need an American look beyond his own country for the sublime and beautiful of natural scenery.[1]

Irving, however, puts against all this the fact that 'Europe held forth all the charms of storied and poetical associations'; besides, though he did not say this, it was really far easier to travel in Europe than in America. England, especially, had splendid roads; America few or none.

'England to an American is not foreign,' wrote the correspondent of the *New York Observer*, in 1831.[2] Americans are the best interpreters of England. No difficulty of language interposes a curtain between them and the English. Both peoples are brought up with the same sort of education; the literature, and to a considerable extent, the history, which young Americans learn, are naturally conducive towards understanding England. In the first half of the nineteenth

---

[1] Washington Irving, *Sketch-Book* (London, 1864), 3.

[2] Colton, *Four Years in Great Britain*, quoted by Spiller, *The American in England*, 362.

century, while immigration was still mainly from Great Britain, the nursery rhymes, pictures, and stories were chiefly English. Therefore the American knew England before he arrived, as indeed the Englishman knew America, though not, perhaps, to the same degree; hence the haunting impression of each on arrival that 'he had seen it before.' Captain Marryat felt this in landing at New York in 1837.

Washington Irving, however, had no particular affinity, by nature or education, with England. He was, indeed, well-read in English literature. The eighteenth-century essayists, Addison and Steele, were perfectly congenial to him. At home in New York he drew his spiritual nurture largely from its Dutch associations and traditions. He was, besides, essentially a man of the eighteenth century, born in the eighteenth century, receiving a good part of his education in it, stroked on the head by George Washington. The genuine eighteenth-century men were cosmopolitans, citizens of the world — Voltaire, Leibniz, Chesterfield, Goldsmith, Burke, Jefferson, Franklin; even Dr. Johnson in spite of his assumption of national prejudice. Irving was a citizen of the world, a freeman, as he liked to remember, of the 'republic of letters,' and in addition almost a career-diplomatist, secretary of legation to the Court of St. James's, Minister to the Court of Madrid — altogether ten years in diplomacy. Therefore he was not particularly interested, as for instance Emerson was, in analysing the English character, describing English traits. England to him was chiefly London, as indeed it was to Emerson, but not for the same reasons: not because the representative Englishmen were to be found there, but because it was one of the centres of the world-republic of letters, just as New York, Boston, and Philadelphia were (though in a less degree), and Paris, Edinburgh, Florence, and Rome. In his sojourns in England (he came three times and spent altogether eleven years there) he showed no interest in politics, or social conditions. He was first and foremost a man of letters who found in England the environment and society which at the time he needed.

The War of 1812–14 between Great Britain and the United States was no sooner over than people 'swarmed' (this was a regular way of expressing it) from both sides over the Atlantic. A regular packet service was now established across the ocean.[1] 'Americans are now treated with the most distinguished kindness and courtesy wherever they are known to be such,' wrote George Ticknor (later Professor at Harvard and author of the *History of Spanish Literature*) from London. The unpleasantness of British travellers in the ensuing twenty years has been exaggerated. 'If only one takes the trouble,' writes their most recent historian, 'to examine the serried shelves of British travels, he will find a surprising amount of honesty, friendliness and generosity in even the one big period during which Tory hostility found unrestrained voice.'[2] British people, on their side, had no complaint to make about

[1] Robert E. Spiller, *The American in England* (1926), Preface.

[2] A. Nevins, *American Social History as Recorded by British Travellers* (1928), Introduction. The Ticknor reference, above, is from the *Life of George Ticknor* (1876), I, 54, letter of May 26, 1815.

the Americans who came to England after the War of 1812–14; but Washington Irving had. He arrived on his first visit in 1815, at Liverpool, and wrote:

> This place swarms with Americans. You never saw a more motley race of beings. Some seem as if just from the woods, and yet stalk about the streets and public places with all the easy nonchalance that they would about their own villages. Nothing can surpass the dauntless independence of all form, ceremony, fashion, or reputation of a downright unsophisticated American.... Let an Englishman talk of Waterloo, they will undoubtedly bring up New Orleans and Plattsburg. A thoroughbred thoroughly appointed soldier is nothing to a Kentucky rifleman.

There were other Americans who had just the right manner.

> Charles [King] is exactly what an American should be abroad: frank, manly and unaffected in his habits and manners, liberal and independent in his opinions, generous and unprejudiced in his sentiments towards other nations, but most loyally attached to his own.[1]

It was at this time that George Ticknor approached Liverpool. A pilot boat brought the news of Napoleon's return from Elba and the restoration of the terrible French Empire. 'Even in this age of tremendous revolutions, we have had none so appalling as this,' wrote Ticknor to his father.[2] The usurper, however, was soon put down, and Americans could continue their travels tranquilly. Ticknor was talking with Lord Byron when the news of Napoleon's defeat at

[1] Quoted by C. D. Warner, *Washington Irving* (American Men of Letters), 100.
[2] *Life of George Ticknor*, I, 49 (May 11, 1815).

Waterloo came in. Byron enquired anxiously if it was true. The news was confirmed. 'I am damned sorry for it,' said Byron.

Washington Irving now (1815) began a five years' stay in London, where he represented the business which he and his brother had been carrying on in New York. He did his business, but his heart was in the square mile around Covent Garden, and eastward to Green Arbour Court and Fleet Street. Later, some of his own countrymen said that he was too much attracted by sympathy with England — a criticism often made later about other Americans; similar criticisms, with equal reason or unreason, have been made of Englishmen. Irving, at any rate, refused a flattering and honourable offer made to the keen young writer by the great John Murray, that he should write for the *Quarterly Review*. The reason given for refusal was that the *Quarterly* 'has always been so hostile to my country.' As a gracious literary personality, clearly American, he captured the English public, but he himself was not captured. He found more eccentricities among the British public than among the American. At Buxton in the Derbyshire Peak district, a frequented watering-place, he writes: 'I no longer wonder at the English being so excellent caricaturists, they have an inexhaustible number and variety of subjects to study from.' He turned gladly from the 'bloated noses' and 'spongy appearance' of the old men of Buxton to the 'wits' (the word still lingered on) of the chop-houses around Covent Garden.

Naturally it required time before he became known

to the best literary society; he was not made a member
of Grillions nor of the Club (Johnson's Club which
still goes on); but the poorer (though not, perhaps, less
happy) quarters of the republic of letters were open to
any member of the craft who had sixpence. Irving was
introduced to a tavern in Covent Garden where there
was a 'club of queer fellows, great resort of small wits,
third-rate actors, and newspaper critics of the theatres.
Anyone can go in on paying a sixpence at the bar for
the use of the club.' This satisfied him. 'For my part,'
he wrote (putting the words into the mouth of the
imaginary Buckthorne), 'I hate your fine dinners;
there's nothing, sir, like the freedom of a chop-house.'
He was a 'laughing philosopher.' 'I'd rather, any time,
have my steak and tankard among my own set, than
drink claret and eat venison with your cursed, civil,
elegant company who never laugh at a good joke from
a poor devil for fear of its being vulgar.' Of course,
being a laughing philosopher, Irving showed equal
adaptability to the elegant, civil company when he met
it, and most of his English years were spent in it. He
was writing the *Sketch-Book* all the time of this first
visit. It was published in the United States in 1819;
and proving itself a success there, was published in
London, at Irving's own expense, in 1820. It was an
immediate success here too. After this Irving was free
of every circle in the English sphere of the republic of
letters.

In 1817 Irving made a tour into the south of Scotland. When he came to Abbotsford, the residence of
Sir Walter Scott whom he had never seen, he stopped his

chaise and modestly sent in his card. The great man came out, preceded and followed by his dogs, greeted Irving warmly, and calmly insisted that the American should stay with him for two or three days. Irving was received into the bosom of the Scott family: 'I soon found myself quite at home,' he wrote, 'and my heart aglow with the cordial welcome I experienced.' Together he and Scott climbed the hills, and discussed the comparative attractions of Scottish and American scenery. In the morning Irving rose early and looked out through the branches of eglantine which spread along the casement of his window. To his surprise he saw Scott (who had probably already written a long chapter of *Rob Roy*) seated on a fragment of stone, chatting with workmen engaged on a new building. 'He appeared like a man of leisure who had nothing to do but to bask in the sunshine and amuse himself.'

The *Sketch-Book*, though it is one of the best things ever written on England, regards chiefly the England of London and Stratford and the country between those two places, though Irving went into Yorkshire, and places Bracebridge Hall there.

Irving, like all thoughtful travellers, had the taste for classic ground. Green Arbour Court in the City of London held his heart. 'It was there that Goldsmith wrote his *Vicar of Wakefield*. I always like to live in literary haunts.' When he began to explore the country, he went to Canonbury Castle, 'the remains of the hunting-seat of Queen Elizabeth'; but 'what gave it particular interest in my eyes was the circumstance that it had been the residence of a poet. It was here Gold-

WASHINGTON IRVING

smith resided when he wrote his *Deserted Village.*'
From there, continues Irving, 'I explored Merry Isling-
ton, ate my solitary dinner at the Black Bull, which
according to tradition was a country-seat of Sir Walter
Raleigh, and would sit and sip my wine, and muse on
old times, in a quaint old room where many a council
had been held.'

This was not very deep in the heart of rural England;
nor indeed were the next lodgings — 'at a small, white-
washed cottage, which stands not far from Hampstead,
just on the brow of a hill, looking over Chalk Farm and
Camden Town, remarkable for the rival houses of Mother Red Cap and Mother Black Cap, and so across
Crackskull Common, to the distant city.' The secret
of the attraction of this cottage was not the view nor
the rusticity, but the fact or legend that Dick Steele
had fled to it to escape his creditors; and that here he
had written 'many numbers of *The Spectator.*' It was
an easy walk to Jack Straw's Castle, the inn on the
ridge between Hampstead Hill and Highgate Hill.
Irving took dinner occasionally at the inn and determined to write a poem on the celebrated highwayman.

Next, having slaked his thirst for London, he es-
sayed to try the Thames Valley, and reached Oxford.
Of course he was impressed. 'Learning here puts on all
its majesty; it is lodged in palaces; it is sanctified by the
sacred ceremonies of religion; it has a pomp and circumstance which powerfully affect the imagination.
When I beheld the clustering spires and pinnacles of
this most august of cities rising from the plain, I hailed
them in my enthusiasm as the points of a diadem which

the nation had placed upon the brows of science.'
For a short time he was captive to the charm of monastic buildings, Gothic quadrangles, solemn halls and
shadowy cloisters. He went to New College Chapel,
heard the fine organ and the swelling choir, saw the
window painted by Sir Joshua Reynolds, strolled in
Addison's walk, lounged in the Bodleian. Irving was
not academic, like Emerson. Oxford was simply for
him a place of beauty and sentiment, with the perennial
appeal of stored-up and living tradition; a place to
visit, to ruminate in, whence to return to London.

Stratford, which was then two, or for most travellers,
perhaps three days from London, was rather a neglected
place. It is curious that Mr. Pickwick, whose travels
are imagined by Dickens to have occurred some ten
years after Irving's, is never taken to Stratford; nor
does Borrow go there in *Lavengro*. Irving seems almost to have begun the vogue of Stratford as a place of
national and cosmopolitan pilgrimage. Evidently he
enjoyed the visit, though he knew not a soul there.
The impression remained vivid with him, on arrival at
the end of a tiresome journey, kicking off his boots,
thrusting his feet into slippers, and stretching himself
before the fire in the Red Horse Inn. He found Shakespeare's house rather ill-cared-for. The church and the
Forest of Arden seemed to recall the memory of Shakespeare best; it was not in Stratford, however, that
Irving found the essential England. Probably this was
really always for him in London; but for a time, at any
rate, he was caught by the charm of country life, and
he was inclined at last to look for the heart of England

there, just as in later life in his own land he took to living not in New York but in a farmhouse up the Hudson.

Irving particularly guards himself against taking
London for England. 'The stranger who would form a
correct opinion of the English character, must not con-
fine his observations to the metropolis. He must go
forth into the country; he must sojourn in villages and
hamlets; he must visit castles, villas, farmhouses and
cottages; he must wander through parks and gardens;
along hedges and green lanes; he must loiter about
country churches; attend wakes and fairs and other
rural festivals.' This is not a bad description of a poet's
England, though it has not a trace of the idea of the
Industrial Revolution which was beginning to blacken
certain portions of the land. Irving does not regard the
English as a race of shopkeepers, traders, or artisans,
but as being 'strongly gifted with the rural feeling.
They possess a quick sensibility to the beauties of
nature, and a keen relish for the pleasures and em-
ployments of the country. This passion seems inherent
in them.' England in fact, if you disregarded the Industrial Revolution, was still feudal. 'The various orders of society are therefore diffused over the whole
surface of the kingdom, and the most retired neigh-
bourhoods afford specimens of the different ranks.'
Following up this feudal train of thought, Irving visits
his friend in Yorkshire whom he calls Squire Bracebridge, and describes the household there. The picture
of Sunday is like that given by Rush a few years earlier
when he describes Lord and Lady Castlereagh and their
twenty-two servants all setting forth from the country-

house at North Cray to go to church, the master and
mistress in front, the servants some twenty or thirty
paces behind. At Squire Bracebridge's the old customs were maintained; and although tea and toast were
permitted at breakfast, ale and beef were what the
Squire preferred. Christmas dinner was served in the
great hall. There was 'an old harper seated on a stool
beside the fireplace.' Roast turkey was apparently considered by the Squire to be a new-fangled dish; instead, there was an 'ancient sirloin,' and a pie decorated
with peacocks' feathers.

Here, then, in Bracebridge Hall, was the real John
Bull: 'A sturdy corpulent fellow in a three-cornered
hat, red waistcoat, leather breeches, and stout oaken
cudgel.' John Bull excels in humour, more than in
wit; is jolly rather than gay; melancholy rather than
morose; can easily be moved to a sudden tear, or surprised into a broad laugh; but he loathes sentiment and
has no turn for light pleasantry. He is loyalty itself,
and will stand by his friend with life and purse, 'however soundly he may be cudgelled.'

In the conduct of affairs John Bull is generous. His
domestic establishment is expensive, because of the
number of retainers kept and the amount of beef and
pudding consumed. 'He is the most punctual and dis-
contented paymaster in the world; drawing his coin
out of his breeches pocket with infinite reluctance; paying to the uttermost farthing; but accompanying every
guinea with a growl.' Mr. Bull's estate is a fine one but
it is now embarrassed. He no longer flourishes his
cudgel and trolls out a stave of a drinking-song; but

goes about 'whistling thoughtfully to himself, with his head drooping down, his cudgel tucked under his arm, and his hand thrust to the bottom of his breeches pockets, which are evidently empty.'

Thus Washington Irving, 'writing in a strange land,' among a people whose recent judgments of his own nation had not been sympathetic, paints, one might almost say lovingly, the English character. Nor was this a peculiar or isolated experience. 'England and London have much more than satisfied my expectations,' was George Ticknor's message to his father and mother at the end of his first visit to the old country. Strange though the land was to these Americans, they came with a congenial and appreciative outlook, and found more poetry there than at Vaucluse, more romance than on the Lake of Lucerne.

A visitor not quite so sympathetic as Irving was James Fenimore Cooper, though he seems to have come to England with the purpose and hope of helping to remove British-American misunderstanding. Born in 1789, brought up at Cooperstown on the Susquehanna in New York State, he had been a Yale undergraduate, a sailor before the mast, a midshipman and finally a lieutenant in the American navy. He had written *The Spy* (1821), *The Pilot* (1823), and *The Last of the Mohicans* (1826). Industrious, observant, imaginative, and furnished with plenty of money, he went forth with his wife and family from Cooperstown, to see the world again, the Continent of Europe, England; and he had a book of travels in his mind, to be completed after the journey, which would check the stupid habit of misrepresentation of America so common in English authors. For some time he resided in Paris, writing, observing, consolidating his political sentiments and prejudices; then, in 1828, he went to England. Samuel Rogers, the prince of breakfast-entertainers, a poet of note, if not of great distinction, *made* Cooper's visit.[1] He was very well treated, met interesting people (it was a highly interesting period of English life and letters), but somehow felt out of touch, repelled. Cooper's countrymen say that he was conceited and irritable. Yet he set out to do away with the misunderstanding of the English and Americans, the two peoples who in those days were so busily discovering each other, not always to their advantage. His work on *England* passed almost unnoticed.

Nevertheless, Cooper's *England* is a significant book. Almost in spite of himself, of his training, his expectations, his temperament, he was finding himself at home all the time. He began with a short visit to London, staying at a hotel in Adams Street, much frequented by Americans. On this occasion he came to the conclusion that 'the English gentleman stands at the head of his class in Christendom.'[2] Then he went to the Continent for a few months. When he came back to England, he was going to set up a regular home with his wife and family.

Being a sailor, he chose to travel by the English steampacket, 'from a latent distrust of Gallic seamanship.' His naval experiences made him somehow ap-

[1] Henry Walcott Boynton, *James Fenimore Cooper* (New York), 1931.
[2] J. F. Cooper, *Recollections of Europe* (1837), I, 97.

preciate England's sea-power; he had already passed
the straits of Dover four times, in 1806 and 1807, during
the Napoleonic War, and once saw about a hundred
English ships in the Downs, most of them cruisers.
The sight of the cliffs of Dover gave him that sudden
home feeling, often mentioned by Americans. 'The
place was crowded with so many recollections from
English history, that even the old chimney-pots, with
which the cliffs had pretty well garnished the place,
had a venerable and attractive look.'[1] The contrast
between the two sides of the Channel was striking:
at Calais, 'politeness, vociferation, snatching, fun,
fraud'; at Dover, 'quiet, sulkiness, extortion, thank
'ees, and half-crowns.' On the whole Cooper preferred
the English way; for a man, provided he will pay, 'gets
his work done with the fewest words.' Wright's Tavern
at Dover charmed him. The silent manner in which the
servants did their several duties was 'an indescribable
luxury.' On the road from Dover to Canterbury there
were not many buildings to be seen, but such as there
were reminded him of 'the small, solid, unpretending,
but comfortable brick abodes that one sees in New
Jersey, Maryland, and Delaware.' The Englishman,
Stratford Canning, when he landed at Annapolis in
1820, made a precisely similar remark about the neat
brick houses, in the Queen Anne style, that he saw
there. The Coopers spent the night at Canterbury.
On rising next morning and looking out of his window,
Cooper saw a gentleman in scarlet coat and hunting

[1] J. F. Cooper, *England, with Sketches of Society in the Metropolis* (1837),
I, 8.

cap mounting horse. On the way from Canterbury to
London, he noticed that the small Kentish country
towns were very like 'Burlington, Trenton, Wilmington, Bristol, Chester.'

Arriving at London, Cooper took a temporary lodging where everything was in perfect order. The comfort
which he enjoyed would have cost, he believed, three
times as much in the United States. Soon the Coopers
regularly settled down in a hired, furnished house in
St. James's Place off St. James's Street. It had a tiny
drawing-room, a dining-room and three bedrooms, and
cost a guinea a day, which included service and cooking. He had no expectation of society, but on the first
morning he went to a bookseller's, much frequented
by Americans, and found several enquiries for him.
Then the celebrated William Godwin, the atheist and
author of *Caleb Williams*, now near the end of his life,
visited him. Next, he was introduced to Samuel Rogers
who lived close to Cooper, in St. James's Place. Rogers's
house was charming, not large, but elegant, tasteful.
On the back it overlooked the Green Park. It was near
the public offices of Whitehall, where cultured civil
servants who took a prominent part in London literary
society lived. It was also near the noblemen's houses
of Piccadilly, where were famous picture-galleries and
libraries. In Rogers's *bijou* house, 'the chef d'œuvre
for the establishment of a bachelor,' as Cooper called
it, were rare books, pictures by old masters, Egyptian
sculptures. Rogers soon had Cooper to one of his
celebrated breakfast-parties, and repeated the invitation many times. On the first occasion Cooper met

Cary, the translator of Dante; on another, Lord John
Russell and Sir James Mackintosh. Soon other people
called on him, men of letters, noblemen. Cooper
engaged a footman, 'a steady, little old man with a red
face and a powdered poll, who appears in black breeches
and coat.' He stood behind Cooper at table and could
just see over his master's shoulder.

Cooper was becoming quite fashionable. He sketches
the great men, or at any rate the great Whig men, of
the time; for no Tory, except Sir Walter Scott, came
to his door. He knew well, however, the Whigs of the
Holland House connection: Lord John Russell, the Reformer, 'a small, quiet man, with an air of ill-health';
Sir James Mackintosh, 'a robust, brawny, negligent
Scot, with a broad accent'; Lord Grey, almost a legend-
ary figure among reforming Whigs. Cooper dined at
Holland House, at Lansdowne House. He observed
the number of pictures, old masters but also fine modern paintings, in the wealthy English houses. In spite
of all this quite remarkable reception, Cooper put it on
record that English society was somewhat formal and
a little eccentric. 'Sitting on the floor, with the foot
in one hand, or suspiciously like a tailor, is by no means
unusual.' If this were customary, it certainly is a
strange thing; even in Washington, however, some
thirty years earlier, Andrew Merry, the English diplomatist, had been ushered into Jefferson's presence and
found the President stretched on a sofa, in a dressing-
gown, and balancing a slipper on the point of his toe.

About the climate, Cooper had not a good word to
say. Nor did he greatly admire the land. 'Whatever

may be said of the beauty of the country in England in particular parts, it scarcely merits its reputation as a whole' — although, he added, none of it is positively ugly, 'a heath or two excepted.' He found the social life exhausting; there was so much eating, the rooms were so small, heated and crowded, that he felt compelled to refuse many invitations. He left England feeling, after all, rather more national than before, a little resentful. 'Heaven bless the *Quarterly Review*,' he writes. 'I do believe the *Quarterly Review* has done more towards alienating the feelings of America from Great Britain than the two wars.' This, he concluded, was a wholesome thing for the 'Young Republic.' Sometimes such impressions are the result of some single, unfortunate experience. Cooper had met the famous, arrogant, self-sufficient, and deadly critic, William Hazlitt, but the American, who was also, perhaps, a little inclined to be self-centred if not arrogant, made no advance to the Englishman, and therefore, as he writes, 'Hazlitt wrote me down a coxcomb.' Nevertheless Cooper's real view of England must be sought in another passage, penned apparently about three-quarters way through his stay in England; he writes that the Englishman and the American are so like each other, and there is so much more pleasure in the interchange of thought when the conversation is carried on in his own language, that the American visitor can enjoy English society to the full.

The trip did Cooper good. He had left the United States a little disappointed, after writing his 'backwoods' novels, because the America which he saw

around him was not the America of Leatherstocking.
The Europe, which he sought, somewhat disappointed
him too. So he returned to his own country with a renewed conviction of her worthiness, and a renewed
confidence in her future; and he stayed at home for
the rest of his time. He was satisfied, so far as a man
of his active and contentious spirit is ever likely to be.
He had still a continuation of his fruitful career of
writing before him. England and the Continent of
Europe, like the backwoods of New York State, and
the high seas which he had sailed as a midshipman,
were a rich romantic experience, food for his busy
mind.

The abounding literary ability and literary curiosity
of New England continually made associations with
the literary life of the old country. The Eastern journals sent special correspondents to England who regaled
their readers in Boston, New York and Philadelphia
with long, leisurely, sympathetic letters from London,
Stratford and Edinburgh. In 1831 the three editors
of the *New York Mirror*, George P. Morris, Theodore
S. Fay and Nathaniel P. Willis, were discussing plans
and policies one evening in Sandy Welsh's oyster
saloon in New York. They decided to send a correspondent to England; and Willis, then aged twenty-five,
was to be the man. 'With $500 in cash and a promise
of ten dollars for each letter published, he left Philadelphia on October 10, 1831.'[1] Willis was the prince
of American journalists in the middle years of the
nineteenth century. His *Pencillings*, contributed from

[1] Spiller, *The American in England*, 364.

England to the *New York Mirror*, are graceful, witty, quaint. He had the best of English literary society — dinner at Lady Blessington's with the young Disraeli, already famous as the author of *Vivian Grey*; breakfast with Charles and Mary Lamb. Willis visited England again in 1837, and married an English girl. Almost forgotten now, he was for thirty years a force in American literature, a graceful interpreter of society, highly appreciated in Great Britain, as in his own country.

VIII

EMERSON AND CARLYLE

In 1833 there came to England America's greatest man
of letters, her most sublime thinker. Emerson, on this
first visit, was only thirty years old. He was absolutely
unknown in Great Britain, and indeed unknown in
America, except in New England Unitarian circles.
There, his sermon on the Lord's Supper, preached in
1832, had aroused deep misgivings among his congregation and had led to his resignation. The young minister belonged outwardly to the best New England
type — tall, with prominent, well-formed features,
thoughtful eyes, a clear voice, a deliberate manner of
expressing himself. Inwardly the eternal fire of genius
burned, not wildly as in Shelley and Byron, but evenly,
powerfully, steadily; he had the ancient Greek sense of
form, the Christian spirit of service. With a good
knowledge of English literature, deeply, if not widely,
read in Latin and Greek (Virgil and Plutarch he knew
particularly well), always thoughtful and observant of
mankind, he had an equipment almost unique for seeing
the inner heart of things; the England he would see

would be something beyond the land of country-houses
and historic market-towns. He knew who were the
most representative men, for like all the scholarly
Americans of that and of a later day, he read the
Edinburgh Review, whose contributors, though anony-
mous, were known. Emerson, like another philosophic
visitor of a similar type, Woodrow Wilson, may be said
almost to have been brought up on the *Edinburgh
Review*.

Emerson was the scholar. He belonged to that race
of men — amiable, observant, reflective, studious, fond
of their fellows, yet always a trifle lonely — who have
wandered across Europe since the early Middle Ages,
delighting in casual conversation, in quiet hours in
libraries, in occasional meals with friends. Ideas, people
(as individuals), the trend of history interest the scholar;
he follows his gleam, and searches (but always rather
tranquilly) for the solution of life's enigma. Places
leave their mark upon him, but as ideas rather than
actual physical sites. 'On looking over the diary of
my journey in 1833, I found nothing to publish in my
memoranda of visits to places.' Yet he had gone
through 'Sicily, Italy and France, and had visited
Malta'; and his classical spirit must have received and
vividly retained deep impressions. Florence he saw
under the best guidance, that of the American sculptor
Greenough; but what was most remarkable in his re-
flections on Florence was that he found there a grand
representative of Englishry. Walter Savage Landor
was living in the villa Gherardesca and entertained
Emerson at dinner and breakfast. Emerson found him

to have 'an English appetite for action and heroes'; and that 'Mr. Landor carries to its height the love of freak which the English delight to indulge.' Landor had the English Whig's admiration for Washington, but he 'undervalued Burke,' and 'pestered' Emerson with the Tory poet Southey; but 'who is Southey?' adds Emerson.

Having found this chip of the old English block in Florence, Emerson came on to London, and landed at the Tower stairs. He experienced that curious home feeling which Englishmen on their side (for instance Stratford Canning, Captain Marryat, E. A. Freeman) have felt when landing at Annapolis, New York, and Boston; yet he stepped ashore in somewhat depressing circumstances. 'It was a dark Sunday morning; there were few people in the streets; and I remember the pleasure of that first walk on English ground, with my companion, an American artist, from the Tower up through Cheapside and the Strand to a house in Russell Square, whither we had been recommended to good chambers. For the first time for many months we were forced to check the saucy habit of travellers' criticism, as we could no longer speak aloud in the streets without being understood.' Then Emerson notes the kindred aspect of things: 'The shop-signs spoke our language, our country-names were on the door-plates; and the public and private buildings wore a more native and wonted front.' This passage of the sympathetic New Englander is almost twin-brother to the description which the unsympathetic Englishman Stratford Canning, as it were in spite of himself, wrote of his impression on landing at Annapolis in 1820: 'I felt myself on landing less among strangers than in the foreign towns of Europe, where other languages were spoken, where buildings unlike our own awakened no sympathies in an English mind, and where the manners and customs of their inhabitants had little or no affinity with those of the British Isles. At Annapolis red-brick houses saluted my eyes, and Saxon words, though uttered with a difference, came home to my ears as if they had followed me across the waters, and were only a trifle the worse for wind and weather.' Emerson found when he landed not exactly the same sort of people as he knew in America, but the people whose prints and pictures he had seen on his nursery walls — 'substantial, respectable, grandfatherly figures, with costume and manners to suit.' [1] So in passing over the gangway from his steamer onto the English quay, 'the American has arrived at the old mansion-house, and finds himself among uncles, aunts and grandsires.'

The first pilgrimage of Emerson in England had three chapters: visits to Coleridge, Carlyle, and Wordsworth. Highgate, where Coleridge lived, was, and still is (though London pressed hard upon it) a charming village on a hill, but Emerson had nothing to say about it. The haunting melancholy beauty of the Lake District, which later made Woodrow Wilson a willing captive for life, called forth no remark of Emerson at this time, though in his account of his second journey

[1] This remark was made by Emerson à propos of his visit to England in 1847; doubtless, he had a similar impression in this, his first visit to England in 1833.

he calls Westmoreland and Cumberland 'a pocket Switzerland.' When he went to Carlyle at Craigenputtock and walked up the hills and looked 'down into Wordsworth's country,' he only seems to have mentioned the view of Criffel because Carlyle pointed it out to him.

The three visits to Coleridge, Carlyle, and Wordsworth were an amazing trilogy for an unknown scholar's wandering year; they were probably due to introductions from Dr. William Ellery Channing, who was well known in English religious and philosophical circles. With Coleridge, however, Emerson really made no spiritual contact, although they were both Unitarians. The great philosopher discoursed, 'like so many printed paragraphs in his book,' making scarcely even a pause in which the American might make a remark. He objected to Channing's Unitarianism, and said that if each were to insist on his faith in England, Coleridge would have 'the hotter side of the faggot'— whatever that meant. Emerson, who liked genuine conversation and not monologues, records that the visit was of no use to him except to satisfy his curiosity.

At Craigenputtock, perhaps because it was so difficult to come at (no stage-coach passing near it), Emerson did indeed notice the 'desolate heathery hills where the lonely scholar nourished his mighty heart.' Emerson's tranquil and optimistic view of mankind was very different from the view of Carlyle, who had finished writing *Sartor Resartus*, was making studies for *The French Revolution*, and was forming himself to be England's great nineteenth-century pessimist. The American's enthusiasm for some well-known men grated on Carlyle; 'when too much praise of any genius annoyed him, he professed hugely to admire the talent shown by his pig,' although 'he still thought man the most plastic little fellow in the planet.' Yet the two scholars found that they had a great deal in common. They went for a long walk over the hills and discoursed on the immortality of the soul.

Carlyle had once thought seriously of migrating to America, and had read and enquired considerably concerning that country. He believed the Americans to be a prosperous people, judging from Stewart's account of the 'Boots' at a hotel in New York who had his own house across the street and dined off roast turkey. They were prosperous but undisciplined; rebellion, he feared, was 'the American principle.' It was usual to consider Shakespeare the great link between the two peoples, but Carlyle, nothing if not original, called Gibbon (in a phrase that was surely much more Emersonian than Carlyle's usual style) 'the splendid bridge between the old world and the new.'

The visit resulted in a remarkable friendship carried on by correspondence for forty years, during which Emerson only once again came to England and visited Carlyle, in 1847. Both men were philosophers and, above all other things, cherished ideas, but delighted also in the craftsmanship of words. Both admired especially Shakespeare and Goethe, and felt strongly the tendency of that age to 'find what they wanted' in German thinking and the German tongue. Both were religious, though scarcely orthodox. 'Christ died upon the tree,' said Carlyle to Emerson: 'that built Dunscore Kirk yonder; that brought you and me together.' They were both prophets, but at this time, 1833, there is no indication that either as yet thought of himself as such. They had one more bond; they liked scholarly company, and were 'academic' in taste and habit, though neither would accept permanent academic employment because of its restraints and curbs, however lightly these may be borne. They had the man-of-letters' appreciation of London, the 'heart of the world,' as Carlyle called it, a place which Emerson felt drawn to also, because like Boston it turned out good men, made possible a regular, scholarly life, and yet was too big to give way to the gossipy parochial habits of even the greatest universities. Carlyle, who suffered from nerves and moodiness, was enchanted with Emerson's sweetness, serenity, and otherworldliness. The American stayed the night in Carlyle's house. They had a great talk that evening. 'Next morning,' wrote Carlyle, 'I saw him go up the hill. I did not go with him to see him descend; I preferred to watch him mount and vanish like an angel.'

With Wordsworth Emerson had a happy meeting at Rydal Mount, which George Ticknor of Harvard had visited fourteen years earlier. The great poet, 'a plain, elderly, white-haired man, not prepossessing, and disfigured by green goggles,' talked with him with great simplicity. It was probably not then a platitude (as it has become by a hundred years of repetition) to remark that American education was superficial, though what Wordsworth can have known about it could not amount to much. 'Schools do no good,' he said. He spoke sensibly about certain vulgarisms which recent writers (especially Mrs. Frances Trollope) had described after their visits to America; that came simply 'from the pioneer state of things.' He did think that America lacked 'a class of men of leisure,' though surely the presence in England of men like Washington Irving, Fenimore Cooper, Emerson, Longfellow, and a host of others, however moderate the means on which they travelled, was proof that leisured Americans of the best kind already existed. Then he rather oddly, although prophetically, remarked that 'they needed a civil war in America, to teach the necessity of knitting the social ties stronger.' The poet recited three unpublished sonnets. Emerson's last vision was 'the old Wordsworth, standing apart, and reciting to me in a garden walk, like a schoolboy declaiming.' 'He made the impression of a narrow and very English mind.' George Ticknor, who visited Wordsworth in 1835, received a similar impression — that Wordsworth's mind was not open to the future, and hardly even to the present. His attachment was to the past. 'He feels the whole matter so deeply and so tenderly that it is not easy to avoid sympathising with him.'

Taken altogether, the first visit of Emerson to England was probably the most satisfying that any American ever made, and the most fortunately directed. The second visit to England in 1847 resulted in a remarkable analysis of 'English Traits.' The voyage in those days was still something formidable. The ship in which Emerson travelled was only one of seven hundred and fifty tons, and it was, he wrote, 'filled with men in ecstasies of terror.' It took fifteen days to cross the Atlantic, although described by Emerson as 'hurrying over these abysses.' ''Tis a good rule,' he wrote, 'in every journey to provide some piece of liberal study to rescue the hours which bad weather, bad company, and taverns steal from the best economist.' He mentions without comment, apparently with approval, among the authors represented in the ship's library Captain Basil Hall, whose book on North America had so offended American susceptibilities twenty years before. The liberal study with which he diverted his mind during the 'long, lack-lustre joyless days' of the voyage was to reflect upon England. He came to the conclusion that Americans were the most suitable, the most understanding visitors to England for many reasons; for one, because 'I think the white path of an Atlantic ship the right avenue to the palace of this sea-faring people.... As we neared land its genius was felt. This was inevitably the British side.'

There can be no doubt that Emerson liked England, found it thoroughly congenial. He mentions, as something at any rate worth quoting, a statement imputed to Alfieri that 'Italy and England are the only countries worth living in: the former, because there Nature vindicates her rights, and triumphs over the evils inflicted by governments; the latter, because art conquers Nature, and transforms a rude uncongenial land into a paradise of comfort and plenty. England is a garden.' He does not mention Jefferson's opinion that if asked to name his favourite country everyone would put his

own first and France second. As a public lecturer
Emerson had to do a good deal of uncomfortable
travelling in America at a time when American hotels,
now so well appointed and comfortable, were rather
poor places; accordingly he greatly appreciated this
visit to England (which was a lecture-tour), where he
travelled 'cushioned and comforted' in every direction,
surveying the pleasant, garden-like country, meeting
cultured men, and having for his news the *Times*,
which was written, he says, by manly, clever, well
bred, and even able men. To supplement the *Times* he
could always have *Punch*, 'equally an expression of
English good sense.' There were other good things in
England. 'It was not too hot nor too cold'; 'there is no
hour in the whole year when one cannot work.' The
island is conveniently situated, 'anchored at the side of
Europe, and right in the heart of the modern world,'
and has geographic centrality and spiritual centrality.
It is true that to Emerson night and day were too nearly
of a colour; and he unaccountably adds, 'It strains the
eyes to read and write.' This, however, is the only
drawback on England's industrial conveniency. A
wise traveller will naturally choose to visit the best of
actual nations; and England is the best of actual
nations. (Emerson says this twice.) The England of
1847 left upon him an impression similar to that which
the United States of 1925 left upon visiting Englishmen,
the impression of 'endless wealth.' Yet he thought also
that British power had reached its apogee, its 'solstice,'
or was 'already declining'— this when the Golden
Age of the mid and later Victorian period was just
dawning!

Emerson's enthusiasm for the English (for it really amounted to this, though expressed very soberly) was at any rate partly owing to the fact that he did not find England foreign. Americans who come to England, he wrote, 'are met by a civilisation already settled and overpowering.' It is, however, their own civilisation also; 'the American is only the continuation of the English genius into new conditions, more or less propitious.' Emerson never counselled the Americans to imitate England. Why should they? Their ancestors had taken English civilisation with them to the New World and there, as Emerson had already declared in his famous *Phi Beta Kappa Address* at Harvard, they could develop their own characteristic culture. Nevertheless essential homogeneity remained. In calculating the number of the British in the total population of the Empire (222,000,000) at 'perhaps' forty millions, he goes on: '*Add the United States of America*, which reckon, exclusive of slaves, 20,000,000 people on a country of 3,000,000 square miles, and in which the foreign element, however considerable, is rapidly assimilated, and you have a population of English descent and language, of 60,000,000 and governing a population of 245,000,000 souls.' The English and American peoples are here considered as together governing other races more than four times their number.

When Emerson approached the subject of the essential traits of the English, he was not at a loss; he could name plenty of traits, but he could not say who 'the indisputable Englishman was.' Nor has anyone else ever been able to answer this question. Emerson

turned over the history of the various races who were
said to make up the English stock; the investigation
did not help him much. And yet 'the indisputable
Englishman was very well marked. He was good-
natured, valorous, refined, manly rather than warlike,
affectionate and domestic': a modern reader at once
recognises in this description Lieutenant Osborne of
Journey's End; Emerson finds the type in Nelson
saying, as he lies just conscious, waiting for death,
'Kiss me, Hardy.' The English feed well, 'live jolly
in the open air,' walk 'with infatuation,' and 'put a
bar of solid sleep between day and day.' They are
hardy and wise — 'only a hardy and wise people could
have made this small territory great.' They have a
singular sense of fairness, deep self-respect, and a
'passion for utility'; they are 'instinct with a spirit of
order.' They have 'good minds' and 'mutual good
understanding.' Emerson 'happened to arrive in
England at the moment of commercial crisis,' but he
conceived no fear for the country: 'it was evident that,
let who fail, England will not.' The *one thing* the
English value is pluck. 'I find the Englishman to be
him of all men who stands firmest in his shoes.' Yet
again, it may be asked, Who are the English? ''Tis a
very restricted nationality.' You can see them by
going to the Royal Academy or the clubs and looking at
the portraits of Englishmen. They are not American,
nor Scottish, nor Irish. You will not find 'the world's
Englishman' even in Yorkshire. The race 'reduces
itself at last to London, that is to those who come and go
thither.' And yet those same English are found every-

where *outside* England, administering one-fifth or one-fourth of the world, and 'homesick to a man.'

It appears that Emerson was not really a 'clubable man,' though he was thoroughly agreeable and companionable. He liked occasional meetings with one or two friends, and he particularly enjoyed talking with eminent persons in society and letters whom he met at Carlyle's house in Cheyne Walk, or at that of Bancroft, the American Minister. Carlyle and Bancroft, themselves men of letters and fond of society, had each quite a *salon*. It was the *salon* which is more sociable and wastes less time rather than the club that Emerson liked. His essay on 'Clubs' in *Society and Solitude* is perhaps the least successful of all his literary efforts. It is an excellent disquisition on the tendency of scholars and in general of men of good will to foregather together; but there is almost nothing at all in it about clubs, and there is no trace of their very individual atmosphere. Nevertheless Emerson while in London in 1847 often walked down St. James's Street and along Pall Mall, and was hospitably given the use of the Athenæum and of the Reform; but he valued this privilege only for the people whom he was thus enabled to meet and see, not because it provided him with another home, and the kind of home atmosphere appropriate to his calling. He mistook the nature of the institution. He held that a club of cultured people was a place where they come together in a group to exchange high thoughts or information; whereas in truth it is a place where a man may have a pleasant meal with a friend, but where he is more likely to go for quiet and silent recreation without being alone. Emerson was no more sure at the Athenæum of finding 'what scholars were abroad after the morning studies' than he was at No. 2000 Tremont Street, Boston.

IX

ACADEMIC LIFE

In no section of the lives of the two nations has contact been more frequent or more enduring than the academic. This is because in the colonial period Americans, though not in great numbers, came, naturally enough, for their education to English colleges; and in the seventeenth and eighteenth centuries there was always a considerable number of English graduates in America. There were, besides, some admirable colleges in the United States, small, not grouped together like the colleges of Oxford and Cambridge, but each cherishing the academic tradition, the ancient and liberal studies, with splendid faithfulness. Graduates of Yale or Harvard, or indeed of any of the old New England colleges, or of William and Mary in Virginia, coming to Oxford or Cambridge in the nineteenth century while these universities were still small in the number of their students, could not merely admire, but felt familiarity and kinship. They belonged to the academic confraternity; they already understood or quickly apprehended the jargon of the English colleges, and would find many things not altogether dissimilar from their own in the rules and regulations. It is true that during the greater part of the nineteenth century Americans who went to complete their higher studies abroad usually chose a German university, as Longfellow chose Göttingen in 1829, and Motley also Göttingen in 1831. All, however, visited Oxford or Cambridge sooner or later; some stayed long enough, and in sufficiently favourable circumstances, to come to know the universities from the inside, as for instance when Emerson made a memorable visit to Arthur Hugh Clough, who was still a Fellow of Oriel, in 1848.

Oxford as Emerson found it was much the same as the Oxford of today; Oxford grows bigger, but the ancient colleges remain almost exactly as they were, and the extra undergraduates are lodged in private houses licensed for this purpose. The rules and habits of life inside college are little altered. Emerson was not dazzled by the splendour of Oxford college life and resources, nor was he perplexed by its ritual and curriculum. His description is one of the best short accounts of Oxford in existence. He came when the 'Oxford Movement' was still a burning question, a theme of essays, speeches, and common-room conversation. Less than three years before Emerson's visit Newman, one of the Oriel Fellows, had been received into the Roman Catholic Church. Others, of whom Clough was one, were thinking of resigning their Fellowships because they were not certain of the grounds of any religious faith at all. Some hankered after Newman's way; they were 'in the mood for making sacrifices for peace of mind,' and apparently would not unwillingly have had the advice of the great American moralist and philosopher; but it was a topic, Emerson hastily adds, on which, 'of course,' he had no counsel to offer. He admired the Fellowship system: 'If a young American, loving learning, and hindered by poverty, were offered a home, a table, the walks, and the library, and a thousand dollars a year as long as he chose to remain a bachelor, he would dance for joy.' Yet he found or heard of many men who were preparing to resign their Fellowships, probably because they wanted to marry. 'They shuddered at the prospect of dying a Fellow.' The marriage disability has since been removed.

The Oxford undergraduates as a whole took more physical exercise than the undergraduates in American colleges, and the same thing can be said today. Emerson compares the American undergraduate a little unfavourably with his Oxford compeer: 'With a hardier habit and resolute gymnastics, with five miles more walking, or five ounces less eating, or with a saddle and gallop of twenty miles a day, with skating and rowing matches, the American would arrive at as robust exegesis, and cheery and hilarious tone. I should be ready to concede these advantages which it would be easy to acquire, if I did not find also that they [the Oxford men] read better than we, and write better.'

Emerson looked through the Oxford examination papers and thought them more severe than the degree tests at Yale and Harvard. He computes very reasonably that Oxford sent out yearly some twenty or thirty very able men, and some three or four hundred well-educated men. He did not, however, allow for the fact that Oxford and Cambridge drew upon the talent of all England, that is, on some twenty-five or thirty million people in a country of an old and settled culture; while the twenty million of American people, many as yet unassimilated to the existing culture, were the field from which the American colleges, numbering probably well over a hundred, had to draw their students. Emerson saw one weakness of the Oxford system — the risk that a Fellowship might become 'a bed of ease.' He overestimated the amount of reading — that is, the intensity of study — of the average undergraduate; and in general he had the tendency of many American visitors, not merely to praise Oxford generously, but somewhat to depreciate the performance or standard of the American college.

One of the great spiritual resources of Oxford, as it is one of its greatest charms, is that the college system, its community life, its leisureliness, have engendered, among dons and among undergraduates, the habit of incessant conversation. This canvassing of each other's minds, this continual interchange of knowledge lightly borne, makes an Oxford common-room an inspiring society. 'The great number of cultivated men,' wrote Emerson in his description of Oxford, 'keep each other up to a high standard.' But they did so at Cambridge, Massachusetts, also. Charles Eliot Norton mentions a dinner-party there in 1853, in Longfellow's house, when there were present Arthur Hugh Clough, Hawthorne, Lowell, Emerson, Longfellow, and Norton himself. It is doubtful whether a finer constellation of talent could have been brought together anywhere at that time.

The American scholar has the habit of following his academic course more leisurely than the Englishman. Not that he is idle. On the contrary, he works most steadily; he has an ideal, a standard of accomplishment, which makes him be in no haste to finish his scholarly task. The Englishman wishes to be more quickly through his academic training, and to go forth to his life's work. He rarely spends more than four years at the university before he begins to earn his living. The American scholar may spend four years as an undergraduate, and four more as a graduate student before he becomes Ph.D.; and not till then is he considered fully qualified to be a teacher or writer of learned works. Following such a course, a young American scholar, a graduate of Yale, entered the English Cambridge in 1840, to spend 'Five years in an English University.'

The name of this excellent student was Charles Astor Bristed. He had destined himself for the career of a clergyman; and judging that this career should not be entered young, he decided, after Yale, to go to England, where he became a Fellow-Commoner of Trinity College, Cambridge. A Fellow-Commoner was an undergraduate member of the college, paying higher fees and enjoying greater privileges than the other undergraduates. They were usually wealthy young men, mainly drawn from the aristocracy; and they wore a silver and blue gown, much admired. Young Mr. Bristed, who was just a good New Englander of moderate means, had chosen to become one of these favoured few (a position, he admits, disproportionate to his means) because he wanted to occupy a good position in the college, to see as much as possible of its life, to know and to be known of a reasonable number of men.

The United States was still the United States of the Peace Societies; the question between Slavery and Abolition was not yet absorbing all the nation's interest and energy. The English and the Americans were still, and were to remain for a good many years yet, in a condition of mutual misunderstanding. Emerson had not yet published *English Traits*. The *Travels* of Captain Hall; the journals and descriptions of Mrs. Trollope and Marryat were still circulating and leaving their poison in the Anglo-American atmosphere.

Bristed was of opinion that the Englishmen of this time rather liked to stir up the spirit of strife and disagreement; but he held also the hopeful view that this was really due to lack of knowledge. He aimed, quite modestly (for, after all, every little helps), at trying to prevent this, or helping to prevent this, by making the American known and his name respected. 'It was partly on this account that I had put myself in a position so disproportionate to my financial resources as that of a Trinity Fellow-Commoner.' Thus did he enter nobly that proud and royal foundation, and view with the sense of membership its majestic courts and gardens. He entered with his eyes open and without unwarranted expectations. He knew 'that as the American admirer of England is sure to get some hard knocks at home, so the American in England is apt to be looked at in a false light by the individuals of a nation to which he is well-disposed.' The citizen of the world who is also a patriot of his own country (the best are such) can only sustain his ideals if he has the spirit of tolerance, if he can still go on appreciating another nation in spite of occasional (and inevitable) disappointment.

Bristed was not dazzled by the splendour and opulence of Trinity, by the immense Cambridge inheritance of five centuries of culture. He did not find the average Cambridge undergraduate to be more advanced in knowledge or experience than the Yale student. The educated New Yorker, Philadelphian, or Bostonian knew French, Spanish, and German 'more fluently than the Englishman of the same age' (indeed they well might do so; how many young Englishmen ever knew French, Spanish, or German at all?). 'The English student of eighteen,' according to Bristed's judgment, 'is more a boy than the American of the same age, in manners, in self-possession, in world-knowledge, in general knowledge of literature even.' Nor were the English, apparently, superior or even equal, in respect to the superficial graces of life. This stranger from Connecticut found the English taste in meat and drink to be 'barbarous.' He was easily able to uphold the reputation of himself and his country by possessing well-cut trousers and a knowledge of certain very special New York dishes and liquids.

Although Verdant Green was an Oxford man, it might be said that Bristed's Cambridge was the Cambridge of Verdant Green, with colleges of reading men and boating men,[1] of men who kept horses and men who hungered in garrets, of bearded undergraduates who played cricket in tall hats and sometimes exchanged witticisms across the counter with a barmaid. Bristed himself played a good deal of billiards, in fact wasted (he says) many hours over 'this fascinating game'; for 'when a young man becomes fairly engaged at billiards, he seldom does anything else very regularly.' Nevertheless he bore an exemplary character with the Trinity dons, for he was a man after the heart of those cultured and serious and not over-energetic gentlemen. He writes: 'The studies which I preferred in just sufficient quantity to amuse and excite without fatiguing me, abundance of good cheer for the body, pleasant literary companions, some reputation for talent obtained by very little exertion — everything combined to put me on excellent terms with myself.' He was on equally good terms with his tutors; for, after all, in spite of a capacity and taste for cultured lounging, Bristed was 'one of the few reading Fellow-Commoners.' It is true that he went to 'wines' (and there were many wine-suppers at Oxford and Cambridge in those days), but he had a strong head, as he naïvely remarks, 'not un-improved by practice'; so by this and by his well-cut trousers (and by a sincere and upright character which wins its way in all circles) he maintained his prestige and that of his country among the gilded Fellow-Commoners

[1] 'Boating-men' practically no longer exist. They were not oarsmen who rowed for their college, but unorganised individuals who took their pleasure and exercise haphazard and singly in skiffs and whiffs and dinghies hired by the hour on the river. Readers of *Tom Brown at Oxford* will be familiar with them.

of Trinity. He knew the reading men too, and nobody admired and understood them better than he — their steady industry, their high culture, their conversation so replete with criticism and judgment, their asceticism and simple living and cleanly dressing, their occasional good dinners 'when an old friend turned up or an examination resulted triumphantly.' Those were the men who having taken a high place in the Final degree examinations, were staying up as graduates and were reading for the Fellowship examinations. Studying hard, engaged in severe intellectual labour, regarding life as mainly work, they nevertheless had their pleasure in college life; and in the Long Vacation found the means as well as the time for 'rambles' in Paris, Belgium, Germany. These men were the 'Hardys' of *Tom Brown at Oxford*; nobody has discerned them more clearly or depicted them more sympathetically than Mr. Bristed of Yale. The counterpart of the men who stay up at Oxford or Cambridge to read for a Fellowship are the American graduates who remain at, or come to, Harvard, Yale, or another, and work for the degree of Ph.D., aiming ultimately at the professorial career. When, however, they at last became Fellows of colleges, the reading men of Oxford and Cambridge developed perhaps a little differently from those of Harvard and Yale. Their lives were a little more secluded, a little easier, better protected, than were those of American professors. Some of the older Fellows (so Bristed thought, and correctly) became somewhat 'rusty'; and in Cambridge itself it was a common opinion that perhaps it was best for a Fellow to leave the university after about seven years, 'unless he is strictly devoted to some purely scientific pursuit.' George Ticknor, Professor of Literature at Harvard, who visited friends at Cambridge and at Oxford in 1846, observed that Cambridge had more 'the air of the world,' and that Oxford was 'very monastic,' although too luxurious for genuine cloisters.[1]

It may be that some remain too long in the university. Concerning the effect, however, of the three or four years of undergraduate residence on a young man's character, Mr. Bristed had not the slightest doubt: 'The great change and improvement effected by a few years of collegiate life was to me one of the first problems connected with the English universities.' Probably there are very few youths who go through those three or four years of community life, disciplined yet free, without leaving it better men than they entered it.

It was probably from Bristed's book that Emerson, partly at any rate, learned about the athletic qualities of the English undergraduate. 'Every Cantab,' writes Bristed, 'takes two hours exercise *per diem*, by walking, riding, rowing, fencing, gymnastics, etc.' In New England, on the other hand, he thought that there were no colleges where the students averaged one hour a day of *real exercise;* their strolling habits were not exercise at all. At Yale, 'the last thing thought of was exercise'; and 'if there is a fifteen-days' prayer-meeting, or a thousand and first new debating society, or a lecture on some *spécialité* which may be of use to half

[1] *Life of George Ticknor* (1876), II, 169-70.

a dozen out of the hundred who attend it, over goes the exercise at once.'

Times are now no doubt changed; but in those days Bristed was quite sure that there was one thing in which the English undergraduates had the advantage. 'They understood how to take care of their health.' It was not that the Cantabs were 'either teetotallers or Grahamites.' There was, it is true, a tradition current in Bristed's time that a total-abstinence society had once been established at Cambridge, and that in three years it increased to two members.

Most extraordinary of all, the English undergraduate studied (and still does so) in the vacation! 'Even so, for you may almost take it as a general rule that college regulations and customs in England are just the reverse of what they are in America.' Bristed stayed up and enjoyed the quiet of the Long Vacation, reading Æschylus and Euripides. He won a scholarship, but was placed only in the Second Class in the Final examinations, the Tripos. Nevertheless, he remained in residence, reading for a Fellowship at Trinity. He read hard, but still found time to be sociable. He often had supper, in vacation, with the dons in their combination-room. There he played whist round the fire with them for shilling points, drinking *bishop* (mulled port), and 'a very enticing mixture called *silky*, the component parts of which, so far as I could judge from internal evidence, appeared to be made of rum and madeira.' If one of his friends gained a First Class, he cheerfully went to the supper-party. One night he went to sup with one Traviss, who 'kept in the third story' in New Court. This is how a guest was greeted in those days:

> 'Ah, Bristed,' and Traviss squeezed my hand with a solemn and business-like affection. 'Just in time. What will you take? Ducks — grilled fowls — lobster *grating*, as our cook calls it. — Lawson, here's a young gentleman will trouble you for some duck. Try some champagne — not so good as you get in America, I'm afraid; we're waiting for free trade.'

Meanwhile, the year 1845 came round. Bristed was still reading for a Fellowship, and was thought to have just a chance for it. He found himself insensibly becoming almost an Englishman. 'News from America began to sound to me like news from abroad.' This was the time when the Oregon question had developed into an acute crisis. Things were looking very black. 'Nothing that our papers or publications *said* seemed half so like war as the silence of the English.' He resolved to leave, and go back to his own country and people, although 'it was like tearing myself up by the roots to leave Cambridge.' Before he left, he led a motion in the Union: 'That the American claims in Oregon are just and reasonable.' The subject was taken up by the undergraduates and was debated quietly and 'in a rational tone, and the majority against us was very small.'

Thenceforward, Bristed's career was that of a cultured American citizen in his own country. He married, settled down, and wrote his books. He was now fairly wealthy, and had several homes. He lived chiefly in his Washington house, distinguished as a man of letters, for his culture, and his hospitality, until his death in 1874.

About twenty years after Bristed left Cambridge, another scholarly American recorded his experiences of Cambridge, England. This was William Everett, son of the Edward Everett who was Minister to the Court of St. James's, President of Harvard, and Secretary of State after Daniel Webster. The son graduated from Harvard in July, 1859, and in the following October went into residence at Trinity College, Cambridge, and remained there until the summer of 1863. It was a period of considerable excitement in England; there occurred a Chinese war, the publication of the resounding theological *Essays and Reviews*, the distress in Lancashire, the seizure of the British mail steamer *Trent* by an American Northern naval captain, the death of the Prince Consort, the marriage of the Prince of Wales. In America there was the Civil War. Everett went home when the war was more than halfway through, although the outlook was desperate; at Quarantine, New York, the news that met him was Lee's advance into Pennsylvania.

Everett believed that political events made more stir in an American than in an English college. 'The monastic seclusion is so great ·that it seemed a greater event to me to change my rooms from letter D, New Court, where I was for two years and a half, to letter I, Old Court, where I ended my course, than for the command of the army to pass from McClellan to Burnside.'

The Civil War period, though a time of tension

between England and America, was also a time of understanding: that is to say, the English, on their side, now had their eyes opened, and began to see the Americans as they really are. The Civil War made everyone in England talk about America and filled every English newspaper with American news. The life of quiet, sociable, cultured students like Bristed and Everett, in an English university, and the sympathetic and illuminating books which they wrote, helped towards a wholesome change of mind in England. 'Our habitual idea of Jonathan,' the English editor of Everett's book confessed, 'was as gross a caricature as the pictures represented to the minds of our grandfathers by the name of Mounseer, or the notion Frenchmen yet have of John Bull.' *Punch* had some time before printed a cartoon representing a tall lanky American undergraduate of Oxford, dressed in stars and stripes, being stopped by the proctor with the words: 'Sir — You are smoking a cigar in the High Street of Oxford,' and answering: 'Guess I could have told you that, old hoss.' Everett, however, writing in 1865, thought that never again was an American likely to be so misrepresented.

His description of English university life is clear, well-informed, accurate. He had the eye of a scholar and, though himself a mathematician, appreciated the old classical culture. 'From the moment that Greek literature arose in England, the English universities claimed it for their own.' He did not fall into the common error of giving Cambridge the monoply of mathematics, and Oxford of classics; but he distinguished, and altogether justly, between their external appearance.

'The two towns are far from being a match. Oxford
is one of the most picturesque of England's old cathedral cities, and one of the most active of its modern
county capitals, situated too on the banks of its noblest
river, in the bosom of a fine range of hills, and in the
immediate vicinity of some of the most beautiful and
famous localities of Britain.... Cambridge, on the contrary, is of all provincial English boroughs the most
insignificant, the dullest, and the ugliest.' Some people
may today find Oxford developing too much along its
line of being a 'modern capital,' and may yearn a little
after Cambridge's old market-town aspect. There is
one Cambridge scene which Mr. Everett places above
anything in Oxford — the walks and lawns that lie
along the river behind St. John's, Trinity, Clare, King's,
and Queens' Colleges, known as the 'Backs.'

> There is nothing of the kind lovelier in England. The
> velvet turf, the ancestral elms and hoary lindens, the long
> vistas of the ancient avenues, the quiet river, its shelving
> banks filled with loiterers, its waters a scene of gay boats,
> and crossed by light, graceful stone bridges; the old halls
> of grey or red or yellow rising here and there, the windows
> peeping out from among the trees, and the openings into
> the old courtyards with their presage of monastic ease and
> learning, the lofty pinnacles of King's o'ertopping all —
> there is no such scene of repose and beauty in Oxford or
> any other place of learning.[1]

All through the nineteenth century and down to the
present time, cultured Americans have come in increasing numbers to Oxford and Cambridge. Some
come as undergraduates, to take the full academic

[1] William Everett, *On the Cam* (1869), 121.

course; others, less favoured by time, to attend a summer school in the Long Vacation; and others, of mature years, merely to see the academic life in action, and somewhat wistfully to try to sense its charm. One philosophic observer, a famous teacher of Harvard, in a long and varied experience of Oxford found its secret, not in the common-rooms and at the high-tables, not in the excellent dinners and interesting conversation of the dons, not even in the lecture-rooms and libraries (all of which he tended to avoid), but in the possibility of enjoying in seclusion 'the intense companionship of the past and of the beautiful.' [1]   Oxford is a place to saunter in; one can sit amid perfect afternoon quiet in a college garden, and see with the living eye the grey towers and battlements which have tranquilly sheltered learning for some seven hundred years; and the men of the past, scholars, statesmen, clergy and the thousands of types of the ancient land, flit through the still quadrangles. But Oxford is not a place of ghosts; and the same philosophic observer, who found there solitude and the companionship of the past, discerned also its other secret, the perennial charm of intensely vivid youth.

The academic life of Great Britain and the United States received a notable reinforcement, early in the twentieth century, through the work of a great practical visionary, Cecil Rhodes. The colossus of South Africa, the dreamer of the British Commonwealth of Nations, had ideas that extended far beyond those units. His conception of society transcended nation and empire. He believed in the value of race. Him-

[1] G. Santayana, *Soliloquies in England* (1922), 6.

self a member of the Nordic race or races, he planned to bring select members of these races together in the greatest Anglo-Saxon centre of education. The will of Cecil Rhodes, who died in 1902, established the Rhodes Trust, a large endowment, to maintain at Oxford students from every British Dominion and colony and, in addition to these, from every State of the United States, and from Germany. There was no narrow nationalism in Cecil Rhodes.

> I also desire to encourage and foster an appreciation of the advantages which I implicitly believe will result from the union of the English-speaking people throughout the world, and to encourage in the students from the United States of North America who will benefit from the American scholarships to be established... at the University of Oxford under this my will an attachment to the country from which they have sprung, but without, I hope, withdrawing them or their sympathies from the land of their adoption or birth.

By this means Oxford, which has probably never been without American students since the middle of the eighteenth century, has now always some two hundred undergraduates, Rhodes Scholars from the United States. Resident in the various colleges, these American undergraduates blend with the rest of the undergraduate body. They contribute to its common life; and, in turn, they too submit to the spell of Oxford. Their studies finished, they return to their own country, with experience widened and deepened, able perhaps to give something to American university life, as they have already given to Oxford.

The musings of an American professor on the Atlantic, homeward bound after four years in a chair at Oxford, express the feelings of a scholar poised between the Old World and the New:

Oxford, with all her diversity, has a sort of inner and corporate wisdom that enables her to ignore unsound advice, to adapt herself to the needs of successive eras, and to save all that is best of the age that is passing for the age that is waiting before.

The voyage is nearing its end, and America lies just below the horizon. Today, I shall once more taste Walt Whitman's 'joy of being tossed in the brave turmoil of these times.' But there will be many moments when I shall regret the soft and sheltered days within Oxford walls, the conversation and the company of the most humane and intelligent group of people I have ever known. My days of wine and roses are over.[1]

[1] S. E. Morison, *Spectator*, Nov. 14, 1925, page 866, written from the *S.S. Winifredian*, at sea.

X

AMERICANS AND ENGLISH IN THE
EIGHTEEN-FIFTIES

I. OPINIONS ON ENGLAND

In one of his most celebrated passages in his greatest oration, Burke said: 'My hold of the colonies is in the close affection which grows from common names, from kindred blood, from similar privileges, and equal protection. These are ties which, though light as air, are strong as links of iron.' Spoken before the great separation of 1775, these words have gone ringing down the ages, and haunt the memory of men. The links, light as air, survived the Revolutionary War, and vibrate to every touch. Yet it was not, perhaps, from the American Consulate at Liverpool that the most sensitive appreciation of these bonds was to be expected.

In the middle of the nineteenth century the relations existing between England and America had reached a condition of poise. The acrimony of the early decades of the century had passed away; there was not as yet the slightest hint of the cordiality which was to come with the late nineties. Meanwhile in the fifties, quietness reigned. The somewhat strong presidency of Polk, when British-American relations had been occasionally exacerbated, was a thing of the past. The War of North and South had not yet come to stir, at any rate a portion of English society into maliciousness. Not many Englishmen were visiting America, though a good many were migrating permanently thither. Few Americans were coming to England or to the Continent. 'The American conquest of Europe' had not begun. This quietude, this absence of movement in the relations of the British and American peoples, was favourable to the genius of the sensitive and proud New Englander, America's finest stylist whom fortune placed in the dingy rooms of the Liverpool Consulate. Nathaniel Hawthorne had been college friend at Bowdoin to Franklin Pierce, who became President of the United States in 1853. Pierce, after much persuasion, induced Hawthorne to accept the position of American Consul at Liverpool. The Consul was already well known as the author of *Twice-Told Tales*, *Tanglewood Tales*, and the *Scarlet Letter*.

Hawthorne provides a good example of the friendly attitude with which, it appears, without exception, Americans approach England. The circumstances were not particularly favourable. The original 'Separatist' Hawthorne who emigrated from Wiltshire to New England, the privateer-skipper of the Revolutionary War, Nathaniel's father, who was a sea-captain in the time of Napoleon, did not supply a naturally pro-English tradition. When Hawthorne came to Liverpool to take up his duties, he found his environment extremely unprepossessing. His office was in 'a shabby and smoke-stained edifice,' situated in 'by no means a polite or elegant portion of England's great commercial city.' He approached it by 'a narrow, ill-lighted staircase,' through 'an equally narrow and ill-lighted passageway.' Being of a fairly tranquil and tolerant disposition, he did not exclaim, as Walter Hines Page did on first seeing his Chancery in London sixty years later: 'How can one live in this hole?' He was drawn, however, to admit that the building opposite, an immense cotton warehouse, was 'a plainer and uglier structure than ever was built in America.' A strong statement.

His son later remembered vividly and with pleasure the family's first resting-place on English soil, 'a hotel in one of the lower streets of the city — gloomy, muddy, grimy, but with the charm that belongs to a first experience of a foreign land.'[1] A few days later they moved to Mrs. Blodgett's boarding-house in Duke Street; and even boarding-house life provided a continual and delightful thrill to the cultured but ingenuous Hawthornes. Julian, at any rate, was certain that this was 'unquestionably the most comfortable, reasonable, hospitable and delightful boarding-house that ever existed before or since; nor has nature been able to afford such another boarding-house keeper as Mrs. Blodgett — so kind, so hearty, so generous, so unobtrusive, so friendly, so motherly. Never, certainly, has the present writer consumed so much food (in

[1] Julian Hawthorne, *Nathaniel Hawthorne and His Wife* (1885), II, 18.

proportion to his weight and size) or of better quality.'
This good lady might have come out of one of Dickens's
novels. She was short and round, rosy, smiling, and
spectacled, had brown curls on each side of her face,
wore a clean white cap and a white apron.

The elder Hawthorne, though not quite so ingenuous
as his son, was contented enough with his quarters.
The company at Mrs. Blodgett's was not highly cultured, but Hawthorne (his son writes) had an hereditary
sympathy with Yankee sea-captains, and found satisfaction in the downright simplicity and sagacity of
their conversation. 'Indisputably,' he remarked, 'these
men are alive, and to an extent to which the Englishman never seems conscious of life.' They carried with
them a smell of tar and bilgewater, and sat of evenings
in the small smoking-room, enveloped in a blue cloud,
and playing euchre with amazing persistency and without gambling. The small boys of the house, always
quick to notice what their elders were doing, soon mas-
tered the mysteries of the game, and occasionally
took a hand in it. Hawthorne also played euchre with
the sea-captains, and laughed immensely at the swift
turns of fortune. His strokes of humour made the sea-
captains haw-haw prodigiously. He enjoyed cards,
played a very good hand at whist, and knew a number
of forgotten card-games which he must have learned at
college. The memory of this lodging was entirely
pleasant. So pleased were the Americans to live in
their 'Old Home,' which was England, that they enjoyed every moment of it; even in the not very
encouraging environment of an average boarding-

house, in the rather squalid neighbourhood of the docks.

Hawthorne had one great friend and tie in England, Dr. Johnson, 'with whose sturdy English character,' he writes, 'I became acquainted at a very early period of my life, through the good offices of Mr. Boswell. In truth he seems as vivid to my recollection, and almost as vivid in his personal aspect to my mind's eye, as the kindly figure of my own grandfather. It is only a solitary child — left much to such wild modes of culture as he chooses for himself while yet ignorant what culture means, standing on tiptoe to pull down books from no very lofty shelf, and then shutting himself up, as it were, between the leaves, going astray through the volume at his own pleasure, and comprehending it rather by his sensibilities and affections than his intellect — that child is the only student that ever gets the sort of intimacy which I am now thinking of, with a literary person.' By study and sympathy Hawthorne had come, as the true historian does, to feel the facts and persons, or certain facts and persons, of the past, to be as real to him as those of the present. Facts, if they are to be real, must 'vibrate in the soul of the historian,' according to Benedetto Croce's phrase. Hawthorne knew England before he came, just as Marryat and Trollope and Freeman, and in one degree or another all English visitors, knew America before they came. After describing certain journeys in England, Hawthorne wrote:

Almost always, in visiting such scenes as I have been attempting to describe, I had a singular sense of having been there before. The ivy-grown English churches (even that of Bebbington, the first that I beheld) were quite as familiar to me, when fresh from home, as the old wooden meeting-house in Salem, which used on wintry sabbaths to be the frozen purgatory of my childhood. This was a bewildering, yet very delightful emotion, fluttering about me like a faint summer wind, and filling my imagination with a thousand half-remembrances, which looked as vivid as sunshine at a side glance, but faded quite away whenever I attempted to define and grasp them.

The explanation of this subtle consciousness of familiarity lies, naturally enough, not in any theory of a previous existence of the traveller, but in the associations of his boyhood and youth: history, fiction, poetry, Shakespeare, *The Pilgrim's Progress*, Boswell, the remarks of parents and teachers, have familiarised most Americans and Englishmen more or less with the land and people to which they are going.

In mid-century England, and probably for a good many years before and after the mid-century, the American seldom felt 'quite as if he were at home'; if he did so, it must be because 'he has ceased to be an American.' There seems always to lurk somewhere, on both sides of the Atlantic, what a recent historian still calls a 'slumbering animosity.' At any moment, this can be aroused by particular circumstances, among many, though not indeed among all, of the citizens of Great Britain and the United States. Hawthorne found this slumbering animosity on the English side. He saw reason to believe that the English would value the regard of the Americans, in fact that they rather yearned after it; but 'they are beset by a curious and inevitable

infelicity, which compels them, as it were, to keep up
what they seem to consider a wholesome bitterness of
feeling between themselves and all other nationalities,
especially that of America. They will never confess it;
nevertheless, it is as essential a tonic to them as their
bitter ale.' This was the reason why an American seldom grew to feel *quite* at home, if he really remained
an American, among the English. On the other hand,
'it requires no long residence to make him love their
island, and appreciate it as thoroughly as they themselves do.' Surely this is the truth of the whole matter,
the 'key' to the locked door of the British-American
problem. The two peoples are not the same, and never
were, at any rate after 1775. There need be no pretence
of feeling literally *at home*, one in the country of the
other; for to be at home would be to lose the *piquancy*,
the delightful and stimulating sense, of being abroad.
On the other hand, for an Englishman, without long
residence, to learn to appreciate the Americans' country and way of life as much as they themselves, is easy
and natural, just as, in Hawthorne's judgment, it is
for Americans to appreciate England. 'I seldom came
into personal relations with an Englishman,' he writes,
'without beginning to like him, and feeling my favourable impression wax stronger with the progress of the
acquaintance. I never stood in an English crowd without being conscious of hereditary sympathies.' This
feeling, which the Englishman in America has also,
need not blind the sympathetic mind to another fact,
present in England in the fifties and probably for the
next two or three decades — 'some acrid quality in the

moral atmosphere of England.' Through this, 'it is undeniable that an American is continually thrown upon his national antagonism.'

It is all to the good that the two quite separate British and American nationalities should be recognised. Prejudices and acrimonies exist within nations and between nations.

> These people [writes Hawthorne of the English] think so loftily of themselves and so contemptuously of everybody else, that it requires more generosity than I possess to keep always in perfectly good humour with them. Jotting down the little acrimonies of the moment in my journal,... it is very possible that I may have said things which a profound observer of national character would hesitate to sanction, though never any, I verily believe, that had not more or less of truth. If they be true, there is no reason in the world why they should not be said. Not an Englishman of them all spared America for courtesy's sake or kindness; nor, in my opinion, would it contribute in the least to our mutual advantage and comfort if we were to besmear one another all over with butter and honey. At any rate, we must not judge of an Englishman's susceptibilities by our own, which, likewise, I trust are of a far less sensitive texture than formerly.

There, then, is the truth. Both nations could frankly and with all the better understanding, recognise each other's virtues and defects, their differences and their common possessions. When the account was cast and the balance struck, it would be found, probably, that the American was more generous in his appreciation, and the Englishman less sensitive in his reaction. 'We in our dry atmosphere,' wrote Hawthorne about the Americans, 'are getting too haggard, nervous, dyspeptic, extenuated, unsubstantial, theoretic, and need to be made grosser. John Bull, on the other hand, has grown bulbous, long-bodied, short-legged, heavy-witted, material, and, in a word, too intensely English.' His heaviness of wit (perhaps slightly exaggerated) has at any rate made him tranquil. The English do not object to being shown Bunker Hill or Trenton; they are moved in seeing Gettysburg or Bull Run, while York-town excites little interest in them one way or the other. Perhaps Hawthorne was right when he said that they are 'a strange race.'

In his unattractive office at Liverpool there stood on the top of the usual consular bookcase (containing dusty sets of United States Statutes) 'a fierce and terrible bust of General Jackson,' in a stiff military tunic and collar, 'frowning forth immitigably at any Englishman who might happen to cross the threshold.' The truculence of the old general's expression, however, was wasted upon 'this stolid and obdurate race of men.' For when an Englishman came into the office, and 'occasionally enquired whom this work of art represented, I was mystified to find that the younger ones had never heard of the battle of New Orleans, and that the elders had either forgotten it altogether, or contrived to misremember, and twist it wrong end foremost into something like an English victory. They have caught from the old Romans (whom they resemble in so many other characteristics) this excellent method of keeping the national glory intact, by sweeping all humiliations and defeats clean out of their memory.' This is not exactly correct. The defeats are on record, and are remembered if mention of them occurs; but they have merely an historical interest for the Englishman; they have happened, that is all. Meanwhile, England goes on, or went on, perhaps rather too reliant on her self-sufficiency. Hawthorne's judgment was, 'If England had been wise enough to twine our new vigour round her ancient strength, her power would have been too firmly established ever to yield, in its due season, to the otherwise immutable law of imperial vicissitude. The earth might then have beheld the intolerable spectacle of a sovereignty and institutions, imperfect, but indestructible.'

2. AN AMERICAN IN ENGLAND IN THE EIGHTEEN-FIFTIES

Hawthorne wrote his book on England, at home in Concord, during the Civil War, 'the hurricane that is sweeping us all along with it, possibly into a limbo where our nation and its polity may be literally the fragments of a shattered dream as any unwritten Romance.' He compiled it from his notebooks, journals carefully kept while in England, in the years 1853–57; yet he never once mentions in *Our Old Home* (though it occurs several times in the journals) the Crimean War, the great European contest in which the English were so long and so tragically engaged. Undoubtedly Hawthorne wished to turn his mind away from war, for the lacerating struggle in the South preyed upon his mind and health. By contrast with the hurricane of the Civil War, with the divided, distracted state of America,

NATHANIEL HAWTHORNE

England stood forth in his consciousness as being compact, so 'provokingly compact,' that she ran no risk of internally being disturbed or divided. The danger was not from division but decay. 'Some time or other — by no irreverent effort of violence, but rather in spite of all pious efforts to uphold a heterogeneous pile of institutions that will have outlasted their utility — at some unexpected moment, there must come a terrible crash.' This would be a picturesque and historic event in the eyes of a sensitive observer. 'The sole reason why I should desire it to happen in my day is, that I might be there to see! But the ruin of my own country is, perhaps, all that I am destined to witness; and that immense catastrophe (though I am strong in the faith that there is a national lifetime of a thousand years in us yet) would serve any man well enough as his final spectacle on earth.' From such a distressing thought, Hawthorne turned with relief to the recollection of his tranquil and garden-like England.

Hawthorne began his survey of England from Liverpool, 'the gateway between the Old World and the New.' As Consul he saw many sides of life. He enforced the law with such clear justice and so much sense that he was never unpopular; but he disliked his office from the first, 'and never came into any good accordance with it.... There was nothing pleasant about the whole affair, except the emoluments.' He was, however, an admirable, hard-working official. Visitors for pleasure were not numerous; but very large numbers of Americans were cast upon the shores of England by business or by chance. 'No people on earth have such vagabond habits as ourselves. The Continental races never travel at all, if they can help it; nor does an Englishman ever think of stirring abroad, unless he has the money to spare, or proposes to bring himself some definite advantage from the journey; but it seemed to me that nothing was more common than for a young American deliberately to spend all his resources in an æsthetic peregrination about Europe, returning with pockets nearly empty to begin the world in earnest.'

The Americans came, indeed, on all sorts of quests, and somehow drifted over the doorway of the Consul's office. One was a printer who had come to England to better himself and 'to see the Old Country,' and had never had money enough to pay his homeward passage. He said meekly but firmly: 'Sir, I had rather be there than here' — *there* was Ninety-Second Street, Philadelphia. Another was a country shopkeeper from Connecticut, 'a queer, stupid, good-natured, fat-faced individual,' dressed in a sky-blue, cutaway coat and mixed trousers, who had come to England to see the Queen. He had sent her a photograph of his family, and she had acknowledged the gift through a secretary. It would have been much better, the Consul felt, if Queen Victoria had not been so courteous as to send a reply and thanks. He thought of asking the American Secretary of State, Mr. Seward at the time of writing, to make diplomatic remonstrances to the British Crown.

The unhappy Connecticut storekeeper had the notion that he was the heir to an English estate, a delusion which was present with many other Americans who applied at the Liverpool Consulate. Mark Twain found a drunken old caretaker on a Mississippi steamboat who had the same mania. 'The cause of this particular insanity,' wrote Hawthorne, 'lies deep in the Anglo-Saxon heart. After all these bloody wars and vindictive animosities, we have still an unspeakable yearning towards England.' The belief of humble American folk in their heirship to an English country-house and estate was merely a particular exaggeration of an old heart-ache and longing. If the English had only been a little more sympathetic to this yearning, it might have influenced American polity 'like the tiller-ropes' of a ship. England took pains to shake the Americans off, but the 'blind, pathetic tendency to wander back again,' remained.

Besides the Americans who came to the Liverpool Consulate, there were many political exiles from other countries who desired passages to the land of freedom. There were many sailors too, complaining of ill-treatment on American ships. Very few of these were American citizens. It is probable that many even of the shipmasters were not American; at any rate there was an obvious diminution of 'that excellent body of respectably educated New England seamen, from the flower of whom the officers used to be recruited,' and of whom the Hawthorne family had itself been a shining example. The Consul occasionally brought before the English courts cases of alleged flagrant ill-treatment on American ships, but the English magistrate generally decided 'that the evidence was too contradictory to authorise the transmission of the accused for trial in America.' The British Secretary of State for Foreign Affairs, Lord John Russell, remonstrated with the American Government on the outrages for which it was responsible before the world. 'The American Secretary of State, old General Cass, responded, with perfectly astounding ignorance of the subject, to the effect that the statement of outrages had probably been exaggerated, that the present laws of the United States were quite adequate to deal with them, and that the interference of the British Minister was uncalled for.'

Hawthorne liked simple pleasures. Often, when one o'clock came, he would put on his hat, leave the office, and take his way through the narrow back streets to a certain baker's shop that he knew of. Here there was a lunch counter at which he could stand up and eat bread and butter and cheese: the best and most inexpensive of meals. He found living in England more expensive than 'at home': meat never below fourteen cents, some kinds twenty cents; no tea below a dollar a pound; grapes a penny apiece. The fruit was not as good as in America. 'England cannot grow fruit, with a sun crying its eyes out every day.' [1] Hawthorne had not, at first, a very high opinion of the English climate (though he changed his mind about it later) and occasionally he became a little dejected. One day Mr. Bennoch found Hawthorne at Rock Park (the house he rented at Liverpool) prodding the black coals in a disheartened fashion. Bennoch seized the poker and with vigorous thrusts brought forth 'a rustling luxuriance of brilliant flame.' 'That's the way to get the warmth

[1] Julian Hawthorne, op. cit., II, 31.

out of an English fire,' cried Mr. Bennoch, 'and that's the way to get the warmth out of an English heart too! Treat us like that, my dear sir, and you'll find us all good fellows.' Hereupon Hawthorne brightened up jovially as the fire, and (as Mr. Bennoch thinks) thought better of England ever after.

The enduring appeal to Americans in England lies in the people and in the country. People have virtues and defects. In the meetings of strangers, and even of friends, much depends upon chance and circumstance. On the whole English and Americans have been pleased with the people whom they have met in the others' country. Towards the American country itself, the scenery and the human adaptation of it, English travellers have sometimes been critical — for instance, in the well-known remarks of Captain Marryat on the Mississippi. Since they became aware of the beauty and grandeur of the scenery of the United States, no Englishman's imagination and pen have been able to rise to the occasion and do it justice in description. Americans, on the other hand, have provided the most sensitive, the most justly appreciative, descriptions of the scenery of England. The rare beauty of the English scene consists, or consisted, in a 'perfect balance between man and nature' — the result of an old civilisation progressing, until recent times, by easy and slow stages. This balance between man and nature was conspicuously absent in the vast territory of the United States, where man was busily engaged in overcoming nature and dominating a continent. Just for this very reason, the American, who, from the stories and pictures in his nursery and schoolroom, had always in his mind an impression of the balanced English scene, was peculiarly, uniquely, Hawthorne thought, fitted to appreciate it. Hawthorne saw this 'influence of hoar antiquity, lingering unto the present daylight,' throughout the English scene. 'It is only an American who can feel it; and even he begins to find himself growing insensible to its effect, after a long residence in England.'

There is, naturally, no question of any preference in the American's mind between the scenery of the two countries; everyone likes his own, but should be able to recognise the virtues of another's. Hawthorne boldly compared the scenery of the Old and the New England.

> Any landscape in New England, even the tamest, has a more striking outline, and besides would have its blue eyes open in those lakelets that we encounter almost from mile to mile at home, but of which the Old Country is utterly destitute; or it would smile in our faces through the medium of the wayside brooks that vanish under a low stone arch on one side of the road, and sparkle out again on the other. Neither of these pretty features is often to be found in an English scene. The charm of the latter consists in the rich verdure of the fields, in the stately wayside trees and carefully kept plantations of wood, and in the old and high cultivation that has humanised the very sods by mingling so much of man's toil and care among them.

The old English villages have

> the heavy air of a spot where the forefathers and foremothers have grown up together, intermarried and died, through a long succession of lives, without any intermixture of new elements, till family features and character

are all run in the same inevitable mould. Life is there fossilised in its greenest leaf. The man who died yesterday or ever so long ago walks the village-street today, and chooses the same wife that he married a hundred years since, and must be buried again tomorrow under the same kindred dust that has already covered him half a score of times. The stone threshold of his cottage is worn away with his hob-nailed footsteps, shuffling over it from the reign of the first Plantagenet to that of Victoria. Better than this is the lot of our restless countrymen, whose modern instinct bids them tend always towards 'fresh woods and pastures new.' Rather than such monotony of sluggish ages, loitering on a village green, toiling in hereditary fields, listening to the parson's drone lengthened through centuries in the grey Norman church, let us welcome whatever change may come — change of place, social customs, political institutions, modes of worship — trusting that, if all present things shall vanish, they will but make room for better systems, and for a higher type of man to clothe his life in them, and to fling them off in turn.

The Norman church, its stable tower, its dim and quiet interior, venerable with the consecration of many centuries; the feudal castle, uplifting itself, like Warwick, among stately trees, and rearing its turrets high above their loftiest branches; the Elizabethan villages, with houses of brick and oak, all growing together like the cells of a honeycomb, fronted with a luxuriant and well-trimmed hawthorn hedge, their gardens chock-full of bright-coloured flowers and shrubs of box; — here is the English scene, imagined, however dimly, in the American mind from boyhood, and now, when it is beheld, scarcely to be believed to be real; — so completely does the living picture 'shape out our in-

distinct ideas of the antique time.' Leicester's Hospital
at Warwick, its quaintly gowned pensioners, 'are
shouting across the gulf between our age and Queen
Elizabeth's'; real though they are, we cannot help
feeling that they are on the far side of the gulf. Looking
down on the tranquil river beneath the walls and towers
of Warwick Castle, the reflection in the water seems as
real and tangible as the timeless masonry above.

It might rather seem as if the sleepy river (being Shakespeare's Avon, and often, no doubt, the mirror of his
gorgeous visions) were dreaming now of a lordly residence
that stood here many centuries ago; and this fantasy is
strengthened, when you observe that the image in the
tranquil water has all the distinctness of the actual
structure. Either might be the reflection of the other.
Wherever time has gnawed one of the stones, you see the
mark of his tooth just as plainly in the sunless reflection.
Each is so perfect, that the upper vision seems a castle in
the air, and the lower one an old stronghold of feudalism,
miraculously kept from decay in an enchanted river.

It almost seems that as the English required a Scots-
man, Sir Walter Scott, to interpret their romantic history to them, so they required an American, or more
than one — for instance, Washington Irving and Nathaniel Hawthorne — to interpret their scenery for
them. The American was the ideal interpreter, because
of this strange, half-familiarity that he had with England before he came. Everywhere on the island he saw
things to strike his fancy. Hawthorne had always
thought that the Concord was 'the laziest river in the
world,' but after seeing the Leam at Leamington he
felt that he must 'assign that amiable distinction to the

little English stream.' The pews in Dr. Parr's church at Hatton were 'very like what one may see in a New England meeting-house, though, I think, a little more favourable than those would be to the quiet slumbers of the Hatton farmers and their families.'

He 'already knew London well' before he arrived. Then, soon after coming, he 'had trodden the thronged thoroughfares, the broad, lonely squares, the lanes, alleys and strange labyrinthine courts, the parks, the gardens and enclosures of ancient, studious societies'; and these 'aimless wanderings' confirmed all that he had read of these objects and renowned localities 'which had made London the dream-city of my youth.' In a quiet English garden, in the heart of London, with its glory of verdant lawn, 'the hunger for natural beauty might be satisfied with grass and green leaves for ever'; but the fruit that was raised in the garden was poor. 'For my part,' Hawthorne concludes, 'I never ate an English fruit, raised in the open air, that could compare in flavour with a Yankee turnip.' Curiously, but perhaps correctly, he found that England had the perfect weather. 'Italy has nothing like it, nor America.' At first he had been discouraged, for one of the articles of his office at Liverpool was a barometer, which frequently indicated disagreeable weather, 'so seldom pointing to fair, that I began to consider that portion of its circle as made superfluously.' At Stratford, however, Hawthorne came to a just estimation of the English June, 'the charm of the English summer weather, the really good days of which are the most delightful that mortal man can ever hope to be

favoured with.' Therefore the London garden gave
him days of luxurious idleness, and he did not repent
of a single wasted hour. 'I was as happy in that hospitable garden as the English summer-day was long.'
He experienced a few weeks of 'incomparable summer,
scattered through July and August, and the earlier
portion of September, small in quantity, but exquisite
enough to atone for the whole year's atmospheric
delinquencies.' The perfect days of the Stratford June
and the incomparable summer of July to September in
London seem to be a pretty liberal 'few weeks' for a
much-maligned climate.

The American consular service can have had few
finer types of men than Hawthorne. He himself held
that the men chosen for the work suffered from certain
disabilities. Except for a few brilliant exceptions here
and there, he wrote, 'an American never is thoroughly
qualified for a foreign post, nor has time to make himself so, before the revolution of the political wheel dis-
cards him from his office.' The original appointment
might be unsuitable; and, later, with a change of the
presidency of the United States, the consul would be
displaced, just 'when he might be beginning to ripen
into usefulness.' In Hawthorne's opinion, a great part
of a consul's duty should consist

in building up for himself a recognised position in the
society where he resides, so that his local influence might
be felt on behalf of his own country, and so far as they
are compatible (as they generally are to the utmost extent)
for the interests of both nations. The foreign city should
know that it has a permanent inhabitant and a hearty

well-wisher in him. There are many conjunctures (and one
of them is now upon us)[1] where a long-established, honoured and trusted American citizen, holding a public
position under our government in such a town as Liverpool, might go far towards swaying and directing the
sympathies of the inhabitants. He might throw his own
weight into the balance against mischiefmakers; he might
have set his foot on the first little spark of malignant purpose, which the next wind may blow into a national war.
But we wilfully give up all advantages of this kind. The
position is totally beyond the attainment of an American;
there today, bristling over with the porcupine quills of our
Republic, and gone tomorrow, just as he is becoming
sensible of the broader and more generous patriotism which
might almost amalgamate with that of England, without
losing an atom of its native force and flavour.

A recent state paper (1931) has contrasted 'the old,
genuine patriotism' with 'a narrow national egotism.'
Hawthorne, in the middle of the nineteenth century,
was well aware of the difference; and he knew that
appreciation of another country and people was compatible with the loftiest American patriotism. The
inhabitants of Old Boston in Lincolnshire, which Hawthorne piously went to see, seemed in a dim way to
have the same idea of patriotism too. They had a
Bunker Hill outside the town, and (somewhat to Hawthorne's surprise) were proud that a place in their
neighbourhood had given its name to the United States'
first and most celebrated and best-remembered battle-
field.

[1] The Civil War, in progress when Hawthorne was writing *Our Old Home*
from his journals of ten years before.

3. SOME PERSONALITIES

Hawthorne made a host of friends in England, many of them distinguished people. One of the most helpful, however, was not distinguished. He was just a certain Mr. Henry Bright. 'Bright,' says Hawthorne in his consular experiences, 'was the illumination of my dusky apartment as often as he made his appearance there.' 'Mr. Bright used seldom to sit down, but stood erect on the hearth-rug; tall, slender, good-humoured, laughing, voluble; with his English eyeglass, his English speech, and his English prejudices — certainly one of the most delightfully English Englishmen that ever lived.' [1]

The acquaintance which Hawthorne made with the sons of the poet Burns was, of course, something particularly to remember. It happened at a dinner-party.

> Late in the evening, Mr. Aiken and most of the gentlemen retired to the smoking-room, where we found brandy, whiskey and some good cigars. The sons of the poet showed, I think, a hereditary appreciation of good liquor, both at the dinner-table (where they neglected neither sherry, port, hock, champagne, nor claret) and here in the smoking-room. The Colonel smoked cigars; the Major filled and refilled a German pipe.... I liked them and they liked me.

He came to the conclusion that the worst of an Englishman is his outside, and that to know him better is to like him better too.

[1] Julian Hawthorne, *op. cit.*, II, 21.

In those days Samuel Warren, the author of *Ten Thousand a Year*, was a literary celebrity. It is a pleasant, old-fashioned, leisurely novel, centring round a great law-suit. Hawthorne was not greatly impressed. He describes Samuel Warren, a man about forty-six, 'with a pale, rather thin, intelligent face — American more than English in its aspect.' Warren was Recorder of Hull, but the attorneys kept business from him, because of his book. He took champagne very freely, and liked Americans and felt very kindly towards them; an American had sent him some Catawba champagne.

Another celebrity, now all but forgotten, was Martin Tupper, who had made a tremendous success with a long series of poems called *Proverbial Philosophy*, published in 1838 and the following years. Although quite forgotten now, he was an eminent and remarkable man. He made enormous sums of money by his poetry, invented an improved horseshoe, glass-stopper, and paddle-steamer, and was elected a Fellow of the Royal Society. Hawthorne went down to stay with him near Aldershot. Tupper had a delightful house in the middle of the village of Albury. The poet took Hawthorne all over and round the house which he insisted courteously had *seven gables*, though the author of that novel could not see as many. The hall of the house had fine old cabinets and ancestral portraits. Breakfast was about to start when Hawthorne arrived. He had already eaten two chops, but he sat down at table. There were seven children, and Mrs. Tupper, and Tupper *père*, who basked in the warmth of his admiring family. He had no dignity, but was a very good man. 'I liked him,' wrote Hawthorne, 'and laughed in my sleeve at him, and was utterly weary of him, for certainly he is the ass of asses. Yet the *Crock of Gold* is a very powerful tale.' They dined early, 'with the whole brood of children,' and the patriarchal Tupper chatting away all the time during the meal. Hawthorne's description is a little unkind to his host, who was not merely a popular poet, but bred horses and, as Hawthorne testified, rode pretty well.

Hawthorne was a good deal in London, and met Charles Reade, the author of *The Cloister and the Hearth*, at the house of Mr. Dallis in Park Lane; he was not impressed by Charles Reade, who was apparently a very much self-satisfied man. He dined at the Reform Club with Dr. Moseley, a Fellow of Oriel and historian of the Oxford Movement. One way and another, Hawthorne seems to have seen a good deal of the Reform Club, though he did not become as familiar with it as Motley did with the Athenæum.

The company which Motley met in London in those days was pretty good. There was Sir James Mackintosh (whom he had already known in America); Lord Houghton, Thackeray, Macaulay; Layard, the traveller to Nineveh; Reeve, editor of the *Edinburgh Review*; Sir Charles Lyell, the geologist; Dean Milman, author of the *History of Latin Christianity*. Motley found Macaulay's conversation (a sort of commanding monologue) rather a severe trial. He quotes Sydney Smith, who said that Macaulay was 'the greatest engine of social oppression in England.' This sort of conversation

could not compare with his friend Holmes's 'ever
bubbling wit, imagination, enthusiasm, arabesque-
ness'; it was 'the perfection of the commonplace.'
Even Thackeray did not impress Motley enormously.
He attended one of Thackeray's lectures on *The Four
Georges* (the lecture on George III), delivered at Lady
Stanley's house; he found it to be graceful and superficial, 'the perfection of lecturing to high-bred audi-
ences.' At one of the Russell Sturgis dinner-parties,
at which both Thackeray and Motley were present,
Thackeray kept on saying at table to his host: 'I hate
that woman,' referring to one of the guests, who seemed
quite inoffensive. He left the party early, 'to work on
The Virginians.'

Thackeray had a more genial mood than this, however, for he was essentially what Dr. Johnson would
have called a clubable man. A year or two before
Motley's visit, he had entertained James Russell Lowell, who described the evening in a letter to Charles
Eliot Norton.

> Thackeray gave us (Story, Cranch — whom I brought
> over from Paris — and me) a dinner at the Garrick Club.
> The place is full of pictures of actors and actresses, some
> of them admirable — one of Garrick as Macbeth, for ex-
> ample — especially those by Zoffany. The dinner was very
> funny. Thackeray had ordered it for *two*, and was afraid
> there would not be enough — an apprehension which he
> expressed very forcibly to the waiter. He said something
> to Story which pleased me wonderfully. There were some
> cutlets which *did* look rather small. 'Eat one of 'em,
> Story,' said he; 'it will make you feel a little hungry at
> first, but you'll *soon* get over it.' The benevolent tone he

gave to the *soon* was delightfully comic. After dinner we went to a room over the 'Cyder Cellar' to smoke. Thackeray called for a glass of gin and water, and presently sent for the last *Newcomes*, saying that he would read us the death of Colonel Newcome. While he was reading, came in a tall man in his shirt-sleeves, and cried: 'Well, Thackeray I've read your last number. Don't like it. It's a failure. Not so good as the rest!' This was Maurice John O'Connell. Thackeray was not at all disturbed, but sent him off cavalierly![1]

Lowell was only on a short visit to England at this time. He had a lodging at No. 1, Bulstrode Street, out of Welbech Street. His landlady gave him breakfast, and he dined off a chop at the Mitre Tavern, which he asserted to be the best in London. It had been frequented by the great Elizabethan wits and by Dr. Johnson; but the chops were the main thing.

Social life among distinguished people in a great metropolis is very pleasant, but there is pleasure, too, in occasionally escaping from it. Motley was made a member of the Athenæum Club, and found, like other distinguished people, that he could dine there alone, and enjoy his own company. This was in 1857. Ten years later, coming back to London from his ministership in Vienna, he entered the quiet rooms of the Athenæum with a feeling of relief, and found himself at once in 'the Silurian Stratum' of his old acquaintances.[2]

London had a remarkable literary society in the 'fifties. Disraeli was almost equally famous as novelist and statesman. Hawthorne saw him at the House of

[1] To C. E. Norton, Aug. 11, 1855; *Letters of James Russell Lowell* (1894), I, 265–66.

[2] To her second daughter, Sunday, July 14, 1857. *Correspondence*, II, 259.

Commons, and noted: 'He doesn't look as if he had a healthy appetite.' The great man was said 'to spend a long time picking the white hairs from his sable locks.' Hawthorne met a more congenial character, Tom Taylor, dining with an American called Henry Stevens who was in the Library Department of the British Museum. He found Tom Taylor to be sensible and humorous, 'but without originality or much imagination.' Yet this Tom Taylor became editor of *Punch*, wrote *Our American Cousin* (the play that Abraham Lincoln was witnessing when he was assassinated), and on Lincoln's death wrote a poem in *Punch* which interpreted to the Americans the character and achievement of the hero. Alexander Ireland, the author of *Dreamthorpe* and *The Booklover's Enchiridion*, was another of Hawthorne's hosts. Emerson had stayed with Ireland too; he was one of the few men, wrote Hawthorne, who had read Thoreau's books. Ireland spoke of Margaret Fuller and *The Dial*; she was a talented New England authoress, who had helped Garibaldi in the siege of Rome in 1849, and was drowned in a shipwreck with her husband, the Marquis Ossoli, and their only child, in 1850. The breakfasts of Richard Monckton Milnes, afterwards Lord Houghton, were frequent and noted literary events. According to Motley's account, 'breakfast' began at 1 P.M. and went on until 7 o'clock. Hawthorne was asked to Lord Houghton's breakfasts and met George Ticknor, Lord Lansdowne, Florence Nightingale, Robert Browning (whom he 'liked very much'), and Elizabeth Barrett Browning.

All this was a predominantly Whig or Liberal as well
as literary society, and it might be considered brilliant
enough to satisfy the American. Hawthorne approved
of it, yet wrote:

> But on the whole, I think the English Conservatives
> are the men best worth knowing — the Liberals, with all
> their zeal for novelty, originate nothing.... The best thing
> a man born in this island can do is, to eat his beef and
> mutton, and drink his porter and take things as they are.
> ... In this way an Englishman is natural, wholesome and
> good.

During his consulship Hawthorne had a visit from
an American friend, the strange and stirring genius
who wrote *Moby Dick*. These mid-century decades
were a grand period in American literature. One of
the finest of all sea-writers was shaping his genius.
Herman Melville in 1837, after seventeen years of life
in Albany, New York, and on a farm in the Hudson
Valley, went off with a small pack on his back and
a fowling piece under his arm, to join the sailing-ship
Highlander. He was still a landsman, in high-heeled
shoes, a total abstainer, a member of an anti-smoking
society, living the hard life of an American merchant
ship in an unsympathetic crew. He cherished a romantic
idea of England, as described by his father, and as he
sat in the dim 'tween-decks picking oakum he consoled
himself by reciting verses of *Childe Harold*. Landing in
Liverpool he haunted the streets and adjacent fields,
hungrily looking for the England which his imagination
had pictured. There was disappointment because the
house in which his father had stayed, Riddulph's Royal

Hotel, was no more. Yet Liverpool was not unfamiliar, for 'in the main, and apart from its poverty, he found it very much like New York.' [1]

Following on this came three years of voyaging in the Pacific and living in the Marquesas Islands, and at the end a spell of service in the United States Navy. Then, three years of literary work at home near Albany, when he wrote *Typee* and *Omoo*. He married and fixed his household in New York and published *Mardi* and *Redburn*. He sailed to England for the second time (1849), carrying the manuscript of *White Jacket*, his romance of the United States Navy. The seas round England gave him a feeling of home-coming: 'thro' these waters, Blake's and Nelson's ships once sailed.' He felt the lure of London, met publishers and men of letters, Scott's biographer, John Gibson Lockhart, who was editor of the *Edinburgh Review*, Moxon the publisher, Richard Bentley, who gave him £200 for *White Jacket*. In 1850 he was back in America, where he had left his wife and family. He took a farm among the Berkshire Hills; here he cultivated the soil and wrote *Moby Dick*. It was here that he first met Nathaniel Hawthorne, who had published *The Scarlet Letter*, and was then settled at Lenox, Massachusetts. This seems to have been Melville's only friendship, apart from some choice souls whom he had learned to love on whaling ships, in the South Sea Islands, and in his one experience of the United States Navy: and these remained only a memory. 'Ruthless Democrat,' as Melville called himself, he nevertheless admired Hawthorne's 'spontaneous aristo-

[1] Freeman, *Herman Melville* (1928), 18.

cracy of feeling,' which came from the intense cultivation of a superior mind.

In about a year Hawthorne removed from Lenox,
and in 1853 went to his consulate in Liverpool. In 1856
Melville, restless, introspective, feeling the urging
promptings to wander, went off again on his travels —
straight to Liverpool. Hawthorne took him round
Liverpool and Chester. Their friendship was sincere,
yet they scarcely understood each other. Hawthorne,
sensitive though he was to outward impressions, was
nevertheless serene and cheerful, happily poised in
a world of fruitful work and domestic felicity. Melville
was half in, half out of the daily round, with no fixed
beliefs, yet with a mystical apprehension of a spiritual
world, restless, unsatisfied, longing, impelled to wander,
but having lost the spirit of adventure. When Melville
departed, Hawthorne, who was fifteen years older than
his friend, felt somehow puzzled and recorded in his
journal:

> He sailed on Tuesday, leaving a trunk behind him, and
> taking only a carpet bag to hold all his travelling gear.
> This is the next best thing to going naked: and as he wears
> his beard and moustache, and so needs no dressing-case —
> nothing but a tooth-brush — I do not know a more inde-
> pendent personage. He learned his travelling-habits by
> drifting about, all over the South Seas, with no other
> clothes or equipage than a red flannel shirt and a pair of
> duck trousers. Yet we seldom see men of less criticisable
> manners than he.

This was the end of Melville's experiences of England,
a half-home which he yearned for, yet which never

satisfied him; nor indeed did any other part of this world. After wandering from Liverpool to Constantinople, he returned to the United States, subsiding into nineteen years of administrative service as Inspector of Customs at New York. He died in 1891, almost forgotten as an author; but the twentieth century has restored the balance and placed Herman Melville in the great gallery of letters.

Hawthorne returned to Concord in 1860, for he wanted his daughters to grow up in America and his son to have an American education. He meant to return, but the opportunity never came.

XI

ENGLAND DURING THE AMERICAN
CIVIL WAR

THE war between the North and the South was the great tragedy of American history; and while the country was riven by hatred and faction, the attitude of the British people was disappointing. Old animosities or prejudices had not yet died. Some, perhaps many, Americans felt that the Civil War was a great opportunity for Great Britain to offer or to accept friendship; instead, 'the North was left with a bitter sense of wrong and outrage, and the South with a conviction that they had been uselessly deceived and betrayed.' Such at least was Henry Cabot Lodge's view; he was just of age to observe public affairs during the latter part of the Civil War, and he visited England soon afterwards. In Mr. Lodge's opinion England's policy during the Civil War was not deliberate, but was due merely to stupidity.

Even the frankest dispatches of diplomatists and statesmen are marked by a certain degree of reticence.

For gauging their own and public opinion their private letters are the most valuable sources, and these, for the period of the Civil War, have been published. Charles Francis Adams, American Minister to the Court of St. James's, 'sailed for his post in May, 1861, and reached England only to be met by the Queen's proclamation recognising the South as belligerents.' [1]

Naturally, during the war there was not a great number of American travellers in England, nor indeed a great number of English travellers in America. The social and political atmosphere on either side was not comfortable for anyone who came from the other side of the water. Such of the English as had relatives in the United States must have had them mainly in the States of the North; yet on the whole public opinion, the vocal part of public opinion, seems to have been in favour of the South. They were not Tories only who appeared to be pleased at the disruption of the American Union, a disruption which they regarded as a Nemesis for the secession of the American colonies from England in 1775. Whigs or Liberals were inclined to admire the South; Mr. Gladstone declared that Jefferson Davis and the leaders of the South had made or were making not merely an army and a navy, but also — 'what is more than either' — a nation.

Most of the Americans who were in England during the Civil War were officials, like Charles Francis Adams the Minister, and his staff; or they were men holding semi-official positions, like the journalist Thurlow Weed, who was directing propaganda for the Union

[1] W. C. Ford, *A Cycle of Adams Letters* (1921), I, viii.

Government. Even official people, however, have
unofficial contact with society; and their unofficial
correspondence indicates how they gradually discerned
another heart in England than the hard heart which
the first months of the war seemed to show. Something
was done in the early months of the war to explain the
Union position by the historian Motley, who used his
magnificent prose style and his convincing power of
argument in letters to the *Times*. Motley was living
in London, having seen the first edition of his *History
of the United Netherlands* through the press in 1860.
After the war had been going on for some months, he
was appointed American Minister to the Court of
Vienna.

Efforts to win the support of the British public
opinion were put forth on the part of the Union and of
the Confederacy, all through the period of the war, and,
naturally, more in the later stages than the earlier. The
Union propaganda, though less highly organised than
that of the South, was more persuasive and more
effective, because it found a response everywhere in the
fundamentally Liberal sentiment of the English people.
The Southern propagandists, Robert B. Campbell,
formerly United States Consul in London, Hiram
Fuller, a New York newspaper editor, Lucius Q. C.
Lamar, M. F. Maury, a naval officer, had a fair amount
of influence. 'One of the most important of the private
propagandists was John R. Thomson, who was very
pleasant and successful in society, and among literary
people, saw much of Carlyle, visited Tennyson and
more completely exemplified the tradition of the true

Southern gentleman.'[1] All this, however, could not balance the weight of English Liberalism and the ascendancy which New England culture had exercised over English sentiment regarding America in the previous forty years.

The British Government was neutral, and high society, in which the American Minister moved, was neutral too — in attitude if not in spirit. 'We are invited everywhere, and dine out almost every day,' writes Mr. C. F. Adams in the month after his arrival, 'but this brings us no nearer.' 'Everybody is civil, but each one has his own interests in England, so that a stranger is but an outsider at best.' He concludes, in a tone of pessimism, unusual among thoughtful people who study Anglo-American relations: 'After all that may be said, there is not, and cannot be, any assimilation of manners and social habits between Americans and English people.'

This categorical judgment, to the effect that the two peoples are and always will be foreign to each other, must have been due to the circumstances of the Civil War and of England's coldness towards the proud New Englander's country in its deadly crisis. Mr. Adams, as early as June, 1861 (nearly six months before the opening of the 'Trent Affair'), thought that he would have to demand his passports. His eldest son, C. F. Adams, Junior, who was in a lawyer's office in Boston, but was on the point of joining the army, wrote to him: 'The feeling here is very bitter.' There was a possibility of Congress passing discriminating tariff legislation, merely in order to injure England.

[1] Jordan and Pratt, *Europe and the American Civil War* (1931), 171.

After the first pained surprise on learning that England was not enthusiastic for the Union, Mr. Adams began to see a little more clearly. Quite early, June 14, 1861, he wrote to his son who was left behind in Boston, referring to those English who sympathised with the South: 'They are not so powerful as to overbear the general sentiment of the people.' A week later he was writing that the English did not want war, but that it might come through misunderstanding — and the misunderstanding was, he thought, at this time, chiefly due to American mistakes. Henry Adams, who was acting as his father's private secretary, wrote on July 2, 1861, to his brother: 'The English are really on our side'; but 'America seems clean daft. She wants to quarrel with all the world.' In face of England's reasonableness, even humility, 'I cannot imagine why we should keep on sarsing her.' Unfortunately there were two things that seemed, in Mr. Adams's view, to check English good will. One was the Union defeat at Bull Run, when there was a disgraceful panic in the Northern army; the other was the attitude of the English press, which seemed relentlessly unsympathetic towards the Union. The American press reciprocated, and 'savagely' assaulted *The Times*. Not until about twelve months had passed, not until the capture of New Orleans by the Union (May, 1862), did the tone of the English press begin to change.

The society to which the Americans were invited seemed to Mr. Adams to be very dull. 'I have not been to a single entertainment,' he wrote to his son, 'where there was any conversation that I should care to re-

member. This is not much of a record compared with
the early part of the present, or the close of the last
century, with the days of Queen Anne, or of Elizabeth.'
The great object of life in England was 'social position.'
To this end horses, carriages, servants, dinner-parties,
must be as handsome as possible. All this effort was
made, with 'profound gravity.' No wonder society
seemed dull to the Americans. Yet they observed too
that there was sincerity in Mayfair, and 'a studied
avoidance of all appearance of ostentation.' Titles
were not paraded, scarcely ever used. There was some
degree of stiffness, however. 'The Englishman is formal
by nature,' concluded Mr. Adams. It should be noticed,
on the other hand, that Englishmen, probably wrongly,
have sometimes claimed to detect formality in the
American manner. Apparently in the sixties English
and Americans were not finding social contact quite
simple. Few Americans, Mr. Adams wrote, wanted to
settle in England.

As the fall of the first year of the war approached,
something ominous seemed to appear in the political
atmosphere. 'Things here take a turn,' wrote Henry
Adams on September 7, 1861, 'which makes it every
day more probable that we must sooner or later come
into collision with England.' Two months later the
'Trent Affair' came like a bolt from the blue to justify
this prophecy.

All the circumstances are now well known. On
November 7, 1861, a Union cruiser treated a neutral,
'English passenger-ship as English cruisers had some-
times treated neutral American ships during the French

Revolutionary Wars. Two Southern passengers were forcibly taken off the *Trent* by an armed guard from the American cruiser. It seemed impossible — practically it was impossible — for the British Government to do anything else than to demand the restitution of the prisoners and an apology from the Union Government. The tragedy of Mr. Adams's position was that he had to uphold the Union point of view while he privately was convinced without shadow of doubt that the Union point of view was wrong.

The news of the Trent Affair arrived in England on November 25. 'We are dished,' wrote Henry Adams to his brother; 'our position is hopeless.' He felt that there was no use in trying to go on with the representation of the Union in London. 'Our present authorities are very unsuitable persons to conduct a war like this or to remain in the direction of our affairs. It is our ruin. Do not deceive yourself about the position of England. We might have preserved our dignity in many ways without going to war with her.' He thought of going off and taking up his old German student-life again 'as a permanency.' Even the fighting son in America felt that England was being simply pushed by the Union into war. He mournfully saw a prospect of his regiment being sent off to fight England. Against the Southern rebels he would fight with a will; 'they are traitors — but against England, we shall have forced her into a war when she only asked for peace.' Mr. Adams in London could only sadly wonder at the exultation over an affair which looked like becoming 'the final calamity' of the Civil War period. His

secretary-son was blunter in his criticism of Mr. Seward
and the forward members of the American Cabinet.
'What a bloody set of fools they are,' he wrote to his
brother on December 13 (1861). Thurlow Weed, working hard and not unsuccessfully at influencing English
public opinion, was afraid that on the other side of the
water, Congress would 'talk' America into war with
England.

Meanwhile, the United States refused to hand over
the two prisoners, Mason and Slidell, seized from the
Trent. Yet Mr. Adams, though bound to present and
support the American 'case,' knew that Great Britain
could not give way to the American point of view.
'The policy must be disavowed and the men replaced,'
he wrote to Charles Francis Adams, Junior. 'Such is
my understanding of the substance, no matter how
gently the sense may be conveyed. Shall we do either?
For my part I think that justice to our former professions demands it of us.... But my opinion is one thing.
What the delusion of my countrymen is, is another and
very different one. They may regard Messrs. Mason and
Slidell as more precious than all their worldly possessions. May be so. For my part, I would part with them
at a cent apiece.' (December 20, 1861.) A week later
he was writing: 'I think that our stay here is at an end.'
However, diplomacy and statesmanship saved the
situation, just in time. The two Southerners were
given back to Great Britain. Suddenly the atmosphere
in England changed. 'The first effect of the surrender
of Messrs. Mason and Slidell has been extraordinary,'
wrote Mr. Adams to his son on January 10, 1862. 'The

current which ran against us with such extreme violence
six weeks ago, now seems to be going with equal fury
in our favour.' The turn in the tide had come. There
were to be more difficulties between England and America before the Civil War was over, but the worst was
passed.

The Trent Affair, as Henry Adams said, 'destroyed
all our country-visits.' People gave up for a time
inviting the Americans, not out of bad feeling, but 'on
the just supposition that we wouldn't care to go into
society now.' The Americans, however, soon went back
to society. Henry Adams used his club (the St. James's)
a good deal. He found, however, as other Americans
have done, that English club-life is not really very
social. The Englishman talks with such members as he
knew before he joined the club; but mostly he does not
talk at all there. 'Clubland,' however, was interested
in the Civil War; the Americans dined with acquaintances at the Reform, Brooks's, and elsewhere, and
found that they could engage in conversation easily
with Englishmen about the war. Some prominent
Englishmen were very much pro-Union; such were John
Bright, Sir Charles Lyell, and among younger men,
Leslie Stephen. Henry Adams thought that the English
aristocracy were 'unconsciously' against the Union,
but they invited him to their parties and he entered
into the spirit of the company, and even danced a
Scottish reel at the Duchess of Somerset's. Nevertheless, he did not 'go ahead very fast' with English
society, because he had nobody to introduce him to
people of his own age. Such English friends as he had

consoled him by saying that it was the same with them; that 'as a general thing young Englishmen were seldom intimate with anyone unless they had known him three or four years.' 'With the *foreigners*,' remarked Henry Adams naïvely (he was writing to his brother), 'I do much better.' By 'foreigners,' he meant French, Germans, and Italians, his colleagues in the diplomatic corps. As an American, he did not consider himself to be a foreigner in England.

The Trent Affair being over, and settled according to the English point of view, the English were pleased with themselves, 'and pleased with us for having given them the opportunity to be so.' The stalwart friends of America, John Bright and Sir Charles Lyell, had now multitudes of sympathisers. 'John Bright is my favourite Englishman,' wrote the philosophic Henry Adams enthusiastically. On Sunday afternoon, May 16, Henry Adams had just come back to the house in Portland Place from a walk in Hyde Park when his father announced with excitement: 'We've got New Orleans.' Henry and Thurlow Weed at once spread the message through the clubs and newspaper offices. 'Next morning *The Times* came out and gave fairly in that it had been mistaken.' It now looked upon the Civil War as a grand historical tragedy, with fate going against the South.

The Civil War seemed unending; and as the fortune of war oscillated on the far side of the Atlantic, so opinion oscillated in England. The Adamses were no sooner saying that they seemed out of the wood than they found themselves in it again. Collisions inevitably took place on the ocean, owing to American efforts 'to stop all the scandalous voyages to help the rebels, that are made from this island.' 'The American question excites more fear here than ever,' wrote Charles Francis Adams to his son on April 24, 1863. Apparently, the fault was not all on one side. Henry Adams wrote: 'If our people keep cool, I think we can set England straight.' Besides there were many good friends of America in England. 'The majority of people,' Henry Adams told his soldier brother, 'receive us as they would Englishmen, and seem to consider us as such.' Motley, by this time American Minister at Vienna, was over in England early in 1863, doing what he could to help. He went up to the North of England, to the districts of cotton manufactures, and formed a very favourable impression of the state of public opinion. He even thought that the misunderstanding was partly due to the American people themselves. To John Bright he wrote from Rochdale (with a lack of accuracy in the matter of date, remarkable in a great historian): 'Coming down from the War of Independence and from the War of 1815 [sic], there has also been in this country [the United States] a certain jealousy of yours.' He added, referring to the British public: 'The mind of the nation is sound.' To his mother he wrote: 'Meetings are held day by day all over England in which the strongest sympathy is expressed for the United States Government.' From his Vienna Legation, he wrote regretfully to one of his daughters: 'The truth is, that our hostile friends, the English, spoil me for other society. There is nothing like London or England in the social line on the Continent. The Duke of Argyll writes to me pretty constantly, and remains a believer in the justice of our cause, although rather desponding as to the issue; and Mr. John Stuart Mill, who corresponds with me regularly, and is as enthusiastic as I am, tells me that the number of men who agree with him in wishing us success is daily increasing. Among others, he mentioned our old friend, the distinguished Dr. Whewell, Master of Trinity (with whom we stayed three days at Cambridge when I received my honorary degree there), who, he says, is positively rude to those who talk against the North. He won't allow *The Times* to come into his home.' [1]

Minister Adams and his son made numerous visits from London; to Monckton Milnes in Yorkshire — 'a very jolly bachelor party'; dinner with the Duke of Argyll, a warm friend, John Stuart Mill, 'the ablest man in England,' Charles Villiers, and Lord Frederick Cavendish, who was later murdered in Phœnix Park, Dublin; elaborate parties at the Duchess of Somerset's and Duchess of Sutherland's. Tom Hughes was called by Henry Adams 'my friend Tom Brown of Rugby school days'; his enthusiasm for the Union cause was unquenchable and infectious. Monckton Milnes, afterwards Lord Houghton, was 'one of the warmest Americans.' Unforgettable kindness was shown to the Americans by the Gaskells of Wenlock Abbey, where everything brought back memories of monks and mediævalism, and by Cambridge dons. 'I wished to become a Fellow,' Henry Adams confided to his

---

[1] Feb. 17, 1863; Motley was in England in March, 1863. *Correspondence of J. L. Motley*, ed. Curtis (1889), II, 119 ff.

brother, 'but am afraid it couldn't be did.' The Cambridge dons were attractive men; and 'how well they do live,' wrote this somewhat stoical alumnus of Harvard.

Lincoln's proclamation emancipating the slaves, issued on January 1, 1863, enormously aided the current of feeling, which was always running somewhere in England for the Union cause. 'It has done more than all our former victories and all our diplomacy,' wrote Henry Adams (January 23, 1863). There was time for a little useful constructive work to be done, outside war-work. John A. Kasson of Iowa, a United States Congressman, came to England and the Continent with the aim, ultimately successful, of arranging an International Postal Union. W. M. Evarts, a prominent lawyer at the New York Bar (later Secretary of State), came over to England, to see it, and to use his influence on public opinion. It was with Evarts that the enchanting visit to Cambridge was made.

Evarts wore a tall hat tilted backwards at a terribly acute angle, and his whole aspect was that of the American as drawn by cartoonists. His conversation, however, made amends for everything; so that Henry Adams was always glad when Evarts took off his hat and opened his mouth.

The ocean seen from the windows of a friend's house on the cliffs of the South Coast, near Saint Leonards, drew Henry Adams like a magnet, even more than the view from the ridge at Much Wenlock, though he returned there too, lingeringly, years after the Civil War was over. Gradually, however, he came to share Dr.

Johnson's opinion that 'nothing was equal to Fleet Street.' So there he lived happily enough, doing his diplomatic work and studying Tocqueville and J. S. Mill. 'We dawdle along here, going to dinners, races, balls, dropping a mild dew of remonstrance upon the British Government for allowing rebel armaments in their ports; riding in the Parks; dining stray Americans and stately English; and in short, groaning under the fardel of an easy life.' (June 5, 1863.)

At the end of June, 1863, however, Henry Adams reported that high society was moving unequivocally against the Union, although the Court showed marked civility. Even Union victories failed to win favour, and when Henry Adams went with Monckton Milnes to the Cosmopolitan Club after news had come of the fall of Vicksburg, he found the company at dinner 'very cold.' In fact, never since the Trent Affair had ill-feeling shown itself 'so universal and so spiteful as now.' The club of citizens of the world was scarcely true to its name, as on this occasion it showed itself as one of the last strongholds of ancient prejudice. The stalwarts who had stood through thick and thin for the Union cause, John Bright, Tom Hughes, Richard Cobden, Charles Lyell, Leslie Stephen, Monckton Milnes, and many others were winning their way; they were helped by the psychology of victory. 'Even *The Times* is converted,' wrote Henry Adams to his brother, 'and gives us a long leader full of praise of Sherman.'

The psychology of victory also affected Adams himself and, doubtless, all the other Union men in England. 'The name of Sherman has placed us who are abroad

in a very commanding position, and our military reputation is at the head of the nations.' They had now no
'Bull Runs' to explain away or excuse. 'I no longer
feel any dread of conversation about our affairs,' writes
Henry Adams; therefore 'society is much more agreeable now than it used to be.' These Americans liked
the English, too, in spite of the fact, partly because of
the fact, that all was not plain sailing. 'Some day
in America,' Adams had written in 1863, 'I shall aston-
ish myself by defending these people for whom I entertain at present only a profound and lively contempt.'
He had a lovely trip to Italy shortly before the Civil
War was over, 'travelling in all luxury at someone else's
expense,' yet he was thoroughly glad to return to
London. 'The whole [Adams] family, indeed, in all
their character were English through and through, in
nothing more than in their constant growling against
the English' — this is the opinion of their biographer.[1]
When they came to leave (they did not go until 1868),
Henry Adams was depressed. He had recently come
back from Italy, and had gone through his last season.

> London had become his vice. He loved his houses, his
> haunts, his habits, and even his hansom cabs. He loved
> growling like an Englishman, and going into society where
> he knew not a face, and cared not a straw. He lived deep
> into the lives and loves and disappointments of his friends.
> When at last he found himself back again at Liverpool,
> his heart wrenched by the act of parting, he moved
> mechanically, unstrung... he felt no sensation whatever
> in the atmosphere of the British peerage, but mainly an
> habitual dislike to most of the people who frequented their

[1] J. T. Adams, *The Adams Family* (1930), 297.

country-houses; he had become English to the point of sharing their petty social divisions, their dislikes and prejudices against each other; he took England no longer with the awe of the American youth, but with the habit of an old and well worn suit of clothes. As far as he knew, this was all that England meant by social education[1].

[1] *The Education of Henry Adams* (1918), 236.

XII

ON BOTH SIDES OF THE ATLANTIC

THERE have always been, at any rate during the last fifty or sixty years of the nineteenth century, individuals or families with a home on both sides of the Atlantic. English girls married into American families and lived in New York and the great cities of East and West. In the seventies and eighties there were many American brides in English families; and their advent had a marked effect in modifying the somewhat formal ways of mid-Victorian high society. The American brides were beautiful and charming and were not held in an endless chain of position and tradition.[1] There were also Englishmen who were born in America and lived there from time to time, without becoming American citizens; the same is true of a good number of Americans born in England. In 1842 General Lewis Cass made an arrangement with Her Majesty's Government about children of either country born within the jurisdiction of the other. The children, when they arrived at the age of twenty-one, could choose whether to be English or American.

[1] Lord Middleton in *The Times*, February 1, 1932.

Besides Americans born in England, or Englishmen born in America, there have always been many citizens of each country who had powerful interests in the other — bankers and merchants of various kinds, publishers of books, scholars, and various others whose interests were private and personal. There are many instances of such people who crossed the Atlantic nearly every year throughout a great part of their lives, and to whom the country that was not theirs by citizenship was a second home. They did not lose their patriotism thereby, though they gained in width of view. No more stalwart American patriot could be imagined than George Haven Putnam, the publisher, a major in the Union army, a characteristic product of a New York family which had decided views and interests in business, culture, and politics.

Putnam was born in London in 1844. His father, 'the first American publisher to invade London,' had established a branch of his New York house there in 1841, and the family remained in London for seven years. The young Putnam had an English nurse 'who was never wearied of talking of London.' She often took him to Hampstead Heath, a great place for children, near enough to the bad, picturesque times for the nurses there to exchange legends of footpads and highwaymen. Putnam in later life kept these memories green by annual visits to England; and each year as he arrived at Euston or Waterloo he had a rush of homelike reminiscence with 'a whiff of that wonderful compound of soot, fog and roast mutton that go to the making of the atmosphere of London.'

An American, who began life in England and who renewed his association almost annually throughout a long life, knew the country, or some parts of it, perhaps better than many Englishmen. He was politically in advance of the Englishmen, too, for in the middle of the century he found them rather ignorant of American affairs. The Putnam family, while it lived in London, knew 'statesmen and other citizens (a group much smaller sixty-five years ago than it is today) who were prepared to interest themselves in American affairs.' These were probably Cobden and John Bright and a few travellers and writers, such as Anthony Trollope, though he had not yet visited America. The Putnams left London in 1848 — 'the picturesque and inconvenient London of the earlier nineteenth century.' They returned in 1851, the year of the Great Exhibition. This time they landed at Southampton, in an open tug — the liner docks were not yet built. 'Chilling' showers met the family, followed by warm sunshine, emblematic of the warm hospitality they also met. If it was raining at Southampton, it was at any rate not so bad as at Liverpool, where, according to Putnam's reminiscences, 'it usually rains black.'

The journey from Southampton to Waterloo is through the greenest region of green England. 'I doubt,' wrote Putnam, 'whether anywhere in the world is there a verdure of grass and foliage to be compared to that of England for its peculiar charm and for freshness of colour.' The family came back to a London which still had mudflats where is now the broad and paved Embankment; which had Temple Bar dividing

Fleet Street from the Strand; and which had no Holborn Viaduct. They found London polyglot, for the Great Exhibition had brought men of all nations who chattered in their own languages as they went along the streets. This seemed strange to the family from New York, who never heard foreign tongues spoken there. 'In the early fifties, New York could fairly be described as an American, in large part a New England city.' The London women were less well-dressed too than the New Yorkers. New York women obtained a more artistic effect for the money expended than did the English; in this respect Fifth Avenue had a more pleasing aspect than Piccadilly. The United States was leading, too, in yachting. In this year 1851, the *America* crossed the Atlantic and raced at Cowes. The result was, as a celebrated report stated: '*America* first, the rest nowhere.' All the subsequent efforts on the part of the English have failed to recapture the 'America Cup.' On the other hand, there has never been quite such an Exhibition as this, the first International Exhibition of 1851. 'Albert was,' as Putnam concluded, 'very nearly a great man'; he saw through the fallacy that one nation prospers at the expense of another. The British required an International Exhibition, and required also broad-minded American visitors like the Putnam family, to open their eyes. 'The American community that was described in *The Times* or was pictured in *Punch*, was not that of Massachusetts or Connecticut, but of South Carolina and Arkansas'; the selection of news was singularly unintelligent.

The third visit of Mr. Putnam, now nineteen years

of age, was in 1861. He came this time to Bristol after a 'remarkably fast' voyage of eighteen days. The passengers landed at Avonmouth. Putnam was then rowed eight miles up the twisted channel of the river to Bristol. There he shouldered a knapsack and walked to London, reading Frederick Law Olmsted's *Walks and Talks of an American Farmer in England*. Olmsted was a particularly good guide for the young Putnam, for he travelled through England with small expenses, putting up at cheap inns or lodging in cottages.[1]

On arriving at London, Putnam took a room in the Ludgate Hill Coffee-house (this must have been one of the last of the coffee-houses), and had 'a David Copperfieldish feeling' at his first solitary dinner with a waiter all to himself. Soon, he crossed to the Continent, and lived a student-life at Göttingen and Berlin. Next, the Civil War claimed him. When the great struggle was over, the annual visits to England could begin. The good ship which had taken him over in 1860 could no longer carry him; it had been burned by the *Alabama*.

For forty years after the Civil War this ardent American continued his crossings of the Atlantic. New York was his home. The Century Club provided (after his family) his greatest social and intellectual companionship. But next to his family, New York and the Century Club, this large-hearted and large-minded man found two other spiritual homes in Oxford and Cambridge. He appears to have been, literally, at home in every common-room in both the universities,

[1] F. L. Olmsted, *Walks and Talks of an American Farmer in England* (1852).

or at any rate a very familiar guest. Year by year he
continued the association, and added with each generation new friends and new clients, for he was an active
and enterprising publisher. When the European War
broke out in 1914 the annual visits had to stop; so he
wrote his reminiscences in the library of the Commonwealth Club, and composed letters on high politics,
to the newspaper press.

Mr. Putnam was a splendid example of the men who
travelled both for pleasure and for business. The
mercantile and banking communities provided people
who stayed for many years at a time on their opposite
side of the water. Such a man, among Englishmen,
was Lord Ashburton who, when still plain Mr. Alexander Baring, represented the London financial house
of Baring in the United States. Carrying on the business of a mercantile banker, he gained a great knowledge
of American affairs. He married an American girl,
Anne Louisa Bingham of Philadelphia. After the death
of his father in 1810, he became the head of the firm.
He sat in the British House of Commons from 1806
until 1835, when he was raised to the peerage. At the
age of sixty-eight, when he was now a great merchant
prince and a peer of the realm, he was entrusted by
Her Majesty's Government with the special mission to
Washington, designed to bring about a settlement of
the international boundary question, particularly along
the Maine border. The result of this negotiation, celebrated in some histories, unjustly, as the 'champagne'
negotiation, was a treaty, signed June 6, 1842, defining
the boundary between the United States and Canada
as it is at this day.

From the American mercantile and banking community there came notable men like Russell Sturgis and
George Peabody. Russell Sturgis was an American who
engaged in business in China, and subsequently joined
the house of Baring in Lombard Street, London. In
the eighteen-fifties and eighteen-sixties Russell Sturgis
had his English country-house at Walton-on-Thames
and his town-house in Portland Place; one son was at
Oxford, another at Eton, there were a daughter and
the youngest son at home. J. L. Motley was a friend
of the Russell Sturgises, and enjoyed their 'princely
hospitality' (as he called it) both at Portland Place and
also at their magnificent mansion on the river. The
Sturgises were visited in 1867 by the Cabot Lodges;
and the young Henry Cabot Lodge was introduced
by the undergraduate Sturgis to river pleasures, to
rowing, and swimming in those quiet waters. The
stimulus of life in a country not one's own, yet familiar and congenial, produced a high literary activity
among the Russell Sturgises; two of the sons made
their mark as novelists. The effect of life in England
upon the Sturgis family was like the effect of life in
California upon Jack London. The one wrote as an
Englishman in America, the others as Americans in
England, but probably better than they would have
done in their own country.

George Peabody's family originally came from England, from St. Alban's, Hertfordshire. He was born of
poor parents at South Danvers, sixteen miles from
Boston, Massachusetts, in 1795. Working as a boy
in dry-goods stores, he gained experience in the science

of buying and selling. In 1829 he became chief partner
in an important dry-goods business in Baltimore. His
first visit to England was in 1827. Ten years later, he
set up permanently as a merchant-banker in London.
All through the nineteenth century American business
men were establishing themselves in London, and
English business men were establishing themselves in
New York, Chicago, Philadelphia, Baltimore, and San
Francisco. This was not immigration of necessitous
people, but the enlightened choice of men of means
and brains, in whose eyes the economic and social
solidarity of England and America made the political
barriers insignificant.

Opportunity waited upon integrity and enterprise;
George Peabody made a large fortune. He was un-
pretentious, kindly, a man of simple life; and as a
good citizen he was as active and benevolent as Benjamin Franklin. In 1848 the State of Maryland employed him as their agent in very difficult financial
transactions which were necessary for the restoration
of the State's credit. He declined any payment for
his services, and received the warm thanks of the
Maryland Legislature. When the Great Exhibition
of 1851 was preparing in London, and the frugal United
States of those days could not see its way to participat-
ing, he gave the money for setting up an American
section. The opening of the Great Exhibition in the
Crystal Palace in Hyde Park on May 1, 1851, was an
event of world-wide significance. Throughout the summer, international crowds thronged the Crystal Palace.
Peabody celebrated the occasion by giving a dinner to

his American and English friends on the Fourth of July. One result of Englishmen's congenital assurance of their place in history is that they will go to an American Independence Day dinner, if it is likely to be well-provided and not dull, just as readily as they will go to any other banquet. Peabody's Fourth-of-July dinners became annual events, were attended by English and American guests, and were a feature of the London season, promoting good feeling between England and America. J. L. Motley in 1858 describes one of these dinners, given by 'the good old gentleman'; Motley enjoyed himself very much. He was paired off 'with a nice English girl who knew the Sturgises, Thackeray, Dickens and others.' Mr. Peabody's business flourished; he had confidence in the Union Government, and steadily bought its bonds during the Civil War; and, as Waterloo crowned the fortune of the Rothschilds, so Appomattox must have made Mr. Peabody rich beyond the dreams of avarice.

There was, however, nothing of avarice about the quiet and kindly New Englander. All this time Peabody was giving on the grand scale. By nature and upbringing frugal and (he said) inclined to be parsimonious, he remained personally frugal, but became to the rest of mankind bountiful and magnificent, and with an equal hand to both countries. The Peabody Institute at South Danvers (piously renamed Peabody), and at Baltimore; the magnificent Southern Education Fund; the Peabody homes in London (housing, at moderate rentals, some twenty thousand people) are enduring memorials of his royal magnificence. Queen Victoria, herself ever kindly, beneficent, friendly, wished to make the large-hearted American a baronet, and to decorate him with the Grand Cross of the Bath. He declined these honours, and being given choice of rewards, asked for a personal letter from the Queen of England. It is deposited in the Peabody Institute at South Danvers. This noble citizen of America and England died in London on November 4, 1869. His body was taken by a ship of the Royal Navy to America for burial in his native town. To give nobly is a great virtue; to give where help is most likely to be permanently useful enhances the significance of the gift. Unnumbered humble and industrious tenants have benefitted by Peabody's London philanthropy. The Americans of the East, South, and Middle West have been helped by his foundations at home. President Wilson as a student in Baltimore lived opposite the Peabody Institute and used its library. Walter Hines Page was an active worker for the Southern Education Fund. George William Childs, the owner of the *Philadelphia Public Ledger*, was a friend of Peabody. He visited England in 1868, and later presented a Shakespeare Memorial Fountain to Stratford-on-Avon, and in other ways commemorated some of England's greatest men of letters.

These mid-Victorian years, the time of the noble and enlightened Prince Albert, were the era of the Cosmopolitan Club. It was not a club with permanent quarters, a stately mansion in Piccadilly or Pall Mall; it was simply a gathering of men of literary, social and political interests, Englishmen and visitors from other

countries. They met on two evenings a week in a
studio in Charles Street, Berkeley Square. 'The object,'
wrote Motley, 'seems to be to collect noted people
and smoke very bad cigars.' Thackeray cynically told
him that men came to the club in 'white choker,' that
is, in evening dress, so as to give the impression that
they had been dining with the aristocracy.[1] Nevertheless, the Cosmopolitan Club was a sound element in
the social life of London in that fine age before the
Franco-German War. It has vanished; but its colleague,
the Cosmos Club of Washington, permanently established in Dolly Madison's house, continues and
flourishes. In the late seventies (the precise year was
1878) Bret Harte, whose stories of miners in California
were almost classic, came to Europe for good. His
vogue had gone; he could not recapture the old charm;
and he had been finding it very difficult to earn a living
for his wife and family in the United States. President
Hayes offered him the consulship at Crefeld on the
Rhine. Bret Harte spent two years there, not very
happily, alone, and then was transferred to Glasgow.
He found Glasgow (he wrote to his wife) even more
enervating and depressing than Crefeld. Occasionally
he escaped to the house of the Duchess of Albany,
Bestwood Lodge, Nottinghamshire. He had made some
good friends. In 1885 his consulship was at an end,
and he removed permanently to London. He would
have liked his family to come to him in England, but
they were growing up and had their interests in the
United States, except one boy who married and came

[1] *Correspondence of J. L. Motley*, ed. Curtis, I, 226. (May 28, 1858.)

to live in England. Mrs. Harte visited him from time to time; but mostly he was alone, writing assiduously, to meet the relentless need for money to send to America. M. Van de Velde, chancellor of the Belgian Legation in London, was a great friend. The Van de Veldes always had a room ready for him in their refined London and country houses. He stayed with the Marquis of Northampton at Castle Ashby and at Compton Wynyates, and was especially thrilled by sleeping in a room above the drawbridge there. He was a distinctly tired man, however, 'overwritten,' composing 'potboilers' as he called them, though he remained careful and faithful to his classic style. His letters to his wife are kind and serious; affection seems to have been dead on both sides. He worked on steadfastly in his London boarding-house until death came in 1902. The British public was hardly aware that a great writer had passed away in their midst.

Probably the two greatest Americans who made their chief homes in England were Henry James and John Singer Sargent. James was born in Washington Square, New York, in 1843 and was educated at Harvard. He was an American through and through. His style, his plots (so far as his novels had plots), his characters, his humour, show the American creative spirit, its freshness and ingenuity, its careful, classical culture, at the best. Henry James is the continuator of the great New England school which was the glory of American letters in the first half of the nineteenth century. Yet, American though he was to the core, he had the nostalgia for the Old World.

Henry James was something more than an American who through frequent, almost annual, visits found a second home in England. In a sense, England was his first, almost his only, home, although it is doubtful if he ever felt himself to be more than a 'permanent sojourner' there. There were essential features of English life about which, until his mature years, he could know very little. The discerning editor of his *Letters* writes: 'One has only to think of the part played by school and college, by country-homes, by church and politics and professions, to understand how much of the ordinary consciousness was closed to him.'

This man of letters, artist, citizen of the world, American, and Englishman by adoption, did not accept England all at once. He paid two sample visits before he finally settled there, and he fought against an attraction which at first he suspected to be superficial. He landed in England (he had been there once before, as a boy) in 1869, the year in which George Peabody died in London, and in which Longfellow paid his last visit. Henry James was a young man, uncertain of himself, moving about, rather vaguely, in England. He spent some time at Great Malvern (much to the benefit of his health), and visited the wonderful Norton family (from Cambridge, Massachusetts) in London, lodged in Half Moon Street, made a brief journey to Oxford, Cambridge, and one or two of the cathedrals, and then went to the Continent. In 1870 he was back in Cambridge, Massachusetts, working fruitfully, though still in a somewhat 'prentice style, on essays and literary sketches. In 1872 he writes in a letter:

HENRY JAMES

'It's a complex fate being an American, and one of the responsibilities it entails is fighting against a superstitious valuation of Europe.' In this year he visited England again, and after a time passed on to a long year and a half of wandering on the Continent, particularly in Switzerland and Italy. Here, when just thirty years old, and with many years of life before him, he was fortunate to find his theme, which had been dimly taking shape in his mind through the last four or five years. 'The American in Europe was to be his own subject, and he began to make it so.' Yet, though nobody visualised better than he the American communities in Rome, Florence, Geneva, and Paris, he never belonged to them. Returning to Cambridge in 1874 he completed his *Transatlantic Sketches*. In 1875 he was back again in England, and this time for good.

On his first visit, Henry James had, all unconsciously, sounded the old note which seems to echo in the heart of every American on landing. 'I really feel as if I had lived — I don't say a lifetime — but a year in this murky metropolis. I actually believe that this feeling is owing to the singular permanence of the impressions of childhood to which my present experience joins itself on, without a broken link in the chain of sensation.' (March 10, 1869.) Nevertheless, in spite of this haunting sensation of having been there before, this consciousness of finding the congenial country of boyhood's dreams, his attitude was not merely observant but critical. To his mother he writes (still on his first visit): 'You will perhaps fancy that I have been rather stingy-minded towards this wondrous

England, and that I was not taking things in quite the magnanimous and intellectual manner that befits a youth of my birth and breeding. The truth is that the face of things here throws a sensitive American back on himself — back on his prejudices and national passions, and benumbs for a while the faculty of appreciation and the sense of justice.' Henry James's faculty of appreciation, however, was not long in attaining a proper strength and poise. In his mind there took form, and in his pages there assumed shape, not indeed the complete England, but the England of education and refined leisure, and also the people to whom that England owes something of its refinement, the visiting and sojourning Americans.

For the Americans have themselves contributed largely to the charm of England which they themselves so keenly appreciate. As children growing up, many of them, with a nostalgia for England, arriving sympathetically, yet with the keen glance of outside observers, they have caught the elusive charm, embodied it in their literature, and so have in a very real sense helped to hand it on, restored and almost re-created. Georgian England lives more *really* in Washington Irving than in Dickens; and mid-Victorian England would lose much of its genuine literary and artistic aspect without the interpretation and contribution of Charles Eliot Norton and Henry James.

It was indeed a wonderful place, this mid-Victorian England of the seventies and eighties, which these two Americans saw. There were Morris, Burne-Jones, and all their Pre-Raphaelite companions; Carlyle in his latter years, the recognised Sage of Chelsea; Ruskin, creating an ideal world of beauty in the chambers of his mind, and in the glowing paragraphs of his prose; and many men of moderate wealth, rich culture, genuine good will, meeting in literary clubs, dining, talking, adding their contribution to a world that was still socially serene and which had passed through and beyond religious unrest.

Like other Americans of means and leisure who spent much time in England, Henry James had a club. He found, however, as others had done, that he only spoke at his club, the Reform, to people he already knew. He often at the Reform saw John Bright, long before he met and came to know Bright at Lady Rosebery's house, Mentmore. It was certainly not club-life that attracted James to London, 'whither I gravitate,' he writes after returning from Italy in 1877, 'as the place in which on the whole I feel most at home.' He assured Miss Grace Norton that he dined out one hundred and seven times in the winter of 1879. He was made familiar with the astonishing intellectual middle-class life of London in those years. Huxley's perfect family circle; 'Huxley's house,' wrote John Fiske in 1872, 'is the nearest to an earthly paradise of anything I have ever seen.' The great professor and his family entertained their friends at 'high tea' at six-thirty on Sundays. Between Huxley's high teas and George Eliot's afternoon teas and Lord Houghton's breakfasts (which continued from Civil War times until about 1880), Henry James certainly saw a large part of England's intellectual life. George Eliot's Sunday afternoons and

Ruskin's parties were attended by James and also by Charles Eliot Norton. James admired George Eliot's 'delightful expression in her large, long, pale, equine face.' Everyone noticed the harmonious tone of her beautiful low voice. She had a tendency, a trifle self-conscious perhaps, to *aborder* only the highest themes. C. E. Norton described her more precisely: 'Her manner is too intense. She leans over to you till her face is close to yours, and speaks in very low eager tones; nor is her manner perfectly simple.'

It was the Nortons who introduced Henry James to Ruskin. It was a lovely household, based upon good health, beautiful taste, affluence; the servants were well-trained, the furniture was exquisite; the hosts and guests were charming. In Ruskin himself, Norton wrote, 'there is a pleasant readiness of sympathy, and cordial readiness in his manner such as it is rare to find in an Englishman.' Henry James was not so sympathetic: 'I went with several of the Nortons to dine at Ruskin's out of town. This was extremely pleasant. Ruskin himself is a very simple matter. In face, in manner, in talk, in mind, he is weakness pure and simple. I use the word, not invidiously, but scientifically. He has the beauties of his defects; but to see him only confirms the impression given by his writing, that he has been scared back by the grim face of reality into the world of unreason and illusion, and that he wanders there without a compass or a guide — or any light save the fitful flashes of his beautiful genius.' Carlyle thought much better of Ruskin.

The magnificent correspondence of Emerson and

Carlyle was now in progress, and in his last letter to
Emerson (dated April 2, 1872), Carlyle wrote: 'Do you
read Ruskin's *Fors Clavigera*...? If you don't please *do*,
I advise you.... There is nothing going on among us as
notable to me as those fierce lightning-bolts Ruskin
is copiously and desperately pouring into the black
world of anarchy all around him. No other man in
England that I meet has the divine rage against in-
iquity, falseness and baseness that Ruskin has and that
every man ought to have.' With Carlyle, apparently,
James had nothing to do; although living a literary
life in London, going to one hundred and seven dinner-
parties and frequenting the Athenæum and Reform
Clubs, he was outside the orbit of the Sage of Chelsea.
James, in fact, was only settling-in to London and
English society in the last years of Carlyle's life, and
Norton does not seem to have introduced the American
to the terrible old prophet. Norton knew Carlyle fairly
well, and probably (as much as Emerson) was the reason
for Carlyle's leaving his 'Friedrich' Library to Harvard.
He might have taken Henry James with him, but he
did not, for a memorable walk with Carlyle in London,
in the neighbourhood of Buckingham Palace and Hyde
Park, in 1872. 'We parted,' writes Norton, 'at the
corner of Piccadilly, Carlyle to take an omnibus to
Chelsea, I to walk home by bright moonlight across
the Park.' Emerson was in England in this year, 1872,
and visited Carlyle, but James met neither, although
he too was in London. Carlyle died in 1887 (the year
before Emerson died). Norton's famous edition of the
Carlyle-Emerson correspondence found Henry James

out of England on a Sunday, 'strolling about in Milan, drinking in the delicious Italian sun.' All this, he wrote, 'takes me away from Carlyle and from the Annandale view of life' — to which indeed James was not entirely sympathetic. Nevertheless he calls Carlyle one of the greatest of letter-writers, though lacking in serenity and pleasantness.

The England of Henry James is largely though not altogether London, Worcestershire, and Rye. Great Malvern in Worcestershire was, at any rate after London, his first choice, in his early days in England. He viewed with a sort of quiet rapture the good old English 'effects' in Worcestershire — the elm-scattered meadows, the sheep-cropped commons, the high-gabled, heavy-timbered, plastered farmhouses, the stiles leading to delicious meadows, the cathedral of the 'Faithful City' soaring up towards Heaven from the plain. Fond of walking though not a great walker, he enjoyed the unsurpassed opportunities of walking on grass, with wide views, among the Malvern Hills; he climbed the Beacon, and found a breezy world of bounding turf with, he averred, some twenty counties at his feet. He could wander for hours, 'delighting in the great green landscape, as it responds for ever to the cloudy movements of heaven.'

Country-house life in England he appreciated from various sources, most grandly at Mentmore in Hertfordshire. It was the house given Baron Meyer de Rothschild, bequeathed to his daughter, Lady Rosebery. There being absolutely no restriction on the ground of expense, life at Mentmore was probably not quite typical. James, who stayed there in November, 1880, wrote to his mother that there was no one 'very important' in the company, except John Bright and Lord Northbrook, lately Viceroy of India. Millais, the painter, came over for an afternoon, and James had a short walk with him. There were three Derby winners in the stables. The house was described by James as 'a huge modern palace, filled with wonderful objects.' Tea was taken 'in a vast, gorgeous hall, where an upper gallery looks down like the colonnade in Paul Veronese's pictures, and the chairs are all golden thrones, belonging to ancient Doges of Venice.' Henry James retired from the brilliant scene, to commune by his bedroom fire on the fleeting character of earthly possessions, and to describe in a letter the scene which he had left. It had sharpened his desire to distinguish himself by personal achievement, as some sort of reply to the 'atrocious good fortune' of the people among whom he was living. Nevertheless, America did not grow dim by comparison. John Bright reminded him of 'a superior New Englander'; and the fortunate Lord Rosebery, the 'favourite of the Gods' (who knew America well), told him that his ideal of the happy life was that of Cambridge, Massachusetts, 'living like Longfellow.' Perhaps a combination of English and American culture provided as good society as the world could offer.

In his beloved Worcestershire, Henry James joined a party with the Millets, who had made their home there. The party included the three distinguished American painters, Millet, Abbey, and Sargent; two

English painters, Alfred Parsons and Fred Barnard; and two men of letters, the Englishman Edmund Gosse, who had delivered a famous course of literature lectures at Baltimore, and Henry James, whose novel, *The Bostonians*, was then appearing serially in the *Century Magazine* (1885). In five bright weeks of perfect weather, late summer or early autumn, the painters painted and the craftsmen of letters wrote and talked. They walked on the glorious hills, or rowed on the Avon from Evesham to Pershore, and the talk flowed along, enchantingly. Quiller-Couch, at that time a young man recently come down from Oxford, was drawn into James's circle. A literary portent was being discussed. 'It was on an evening of those days,' writes Sir Arthur Quiller-Couch some forty-five years later, 'as I sat by the wine listening reverently, Henry James suddenly and irrelevantly stopped an involved sentence with an "Oh, by the way! Have you heard of a wonderful new man who calls himself, if I remember, Kipling, and seems to me almost, if not absolutely, a portent?"'[1] *Plain Tales from the Hills* had just arrived, in grey paper covers, in England.

A visit to Scotland, to Aberdeenshire, where much of London society migrated at the time of grouse-shooting, showed to Henry James how the amenities of modern civilisation could be combined with the ancient rough life of the North; although there was a certain dullness too in the very perfection of detail. 'The British country-house has at moments, for a cosmopolitan American, an insuperable flatness. On

[1] *The Times*, February 10, 1932.

the other hand, to do it justice, there is no doubt of its being one of the ripest fruits of time — and here in Scotland — where you get the conveniences of Mayfair dovetailed into the romanticism of nature — of the highest results of civilisation.' He had grown very soon to like the English. 'The only thing I'm certain about,' he had written to his mother (from the neutral ground of the Hôtel de l'Europe, Florence) in 1869, 'is that I like them — like them heartily.... They have manners and a language.' He was also critical, however, and was soon writing that never from a single Englishman had he heard the first word of appreciation and enjoyment of the things which he himself found delightful. 'What exasperates you is not that they can't say, but that they wouldn't if they could. Ah! but they are a great people for all that.'

Henry James's attitude towards the English was, in fact, rather like that of Henry Adams, for he wrote (in 1880) to Charles Eliot Norton: 'Considering that I lose all patience with the English about fifteen times a day, and vow that I renounce them for ever, I get on with them beautifully and love them well.' The English mind was fairly simple; he declares that if he had not known it, he could have invented it. He did not feel confident of the country's future, although the public faced problems seriously. England was deeply — 'tragically' — charged with a consciousness of her responsibilities. This was the time when the Eastern Question — Turkey — was absorbing public attention, and when everybody was wondering whether Great Britain would allow the Russians to march to Constantinople. 'I really think that we are assisting at the political decadence of our mighty motherland,' writes the American. '... One has a feeling that the affairs of Europe are going to be settled without her.' (December 15, 1877.) England, however, did show firmness (though, Henry James thought, on the wrong side), and the Congress of Vienna propped up Turkey once more.

Although he said that England was not, and never had been a land of ideas, Henry James was not repelled. And although in 1877, when still only forty-four years old, he had written that he was past the age for forming friendships, he was continually adding to the circle that was attracted by his lovableness. A great friend to him (and also to Theodore Roosevelt) was Sir George Otto Trevelyan, the historian of Charles James Fox and of the American Revolution. In 1904 Sir George wrote from his house, Welcombe, Stratford-on-Avon, to Roosevelt: 'We have just parted from Henry James. He comes to us every year, and is never tired of this beautiful and classical neighbourhood.' In 1913 'three hundred of his English circle' joined together to have his portrait painted by Sargent. For twenty years he lived continuously in England, except for occasional flights to satisfy his 'travelling impulse' on the Continent. Then in 1904 this 'cosmopolitan American,' this internationalist, as he was inclined to consider himself, confessed that at the back of his head and the bottom of his heart, he was 'tremendously homesick.' So for ten months he went to America, saw and visited his many friends, recalled old memories, and admired especially the wonderful and majestic growth of Harvard with 'such a swarm of distinguished specialists and such a big organisation of learning.' He was interested to visit 'the extraordinary colossal French *château* of George Vanderbilt' in the North Carolina mountains, 'of a size to contain two or three Mentmores and Waddesdons.'

As the months went past, he yearned for the peace of Lamb House, Rye, which he had bought eight years before (1896). That pleasant eighteenth-century red-brick house in the quaint old town on the hill had naturally become a literary home; it was dignified and refined, but it was not warm. 'Effective hot-water pipes,' introduced in 1906, brought its temperature to a point perhaps approaching the American standard. 'My poor little house,' he wrote to G. T. Lapsley of Trinity College, Cambridge, 'is now really warm — even hot.' Here he spent most of the rest of his life, with fairly frequent visits to London. Lamb House, had it been in Paris, would have been considered to be the home of a *salon*; for here this master of pure English style gave of his wit and wisdom to kindred spirits; from here he carried on a wide, sympathetic, and lively correspondence. Rye was his home, but London saw him regularly, if not frequently. He found the isolation of London club-life congenial and helpful; he was often seen in the library of the Athenæum and Reform. He liked London even at the week-end, and found the quiet and emptiness of Sunday not unpleasant. (Oliver Wendell Holmes called London on Sunday a city of 'sulky suicide.') [1]

[1] Morse, J. T., *Life and Letters of O. W. Holmes* (1896), I, 132.

The Victorian *social Sunday*, which as a young man he had known and enjoyed in London, was now gone; the cultured bourgeoisie fled to the country on Sunday, or else there were no Huxleys and George Eliots to be at home. Yet, though the glory of the Chelsea, Kensington, or Bloomsbury Sundays had departed, the 'holy stillness' which remained had its merits; so he sat in the great dim solemn library of the club, and wrote his letters, while he waited for a friend to come and dine.

It was in this tranquil, friendly, fruitful existence at Rye and London that the war caught Henry James in his seventy-first year. 'The challenge of the war with Germany roused him to a height of passion he had never touched before in the outer world; and if the strain of it exhausted his strength, as well it might, it gave him one last year of the fullest and deepest experience he had ever known. It wore out his body which was too tired and spent to live longer; but he carried away the power of its spirit in its prime.' [1]

---

[1] From *The Letters of Henry James*, edited by Percy Lubbock (1920), I, xxxi. The quotations of Henry James's letters in the present chapter are from this edition.

XIII

THE LATER ARTISTS

WEST and Copley made notable contributions to English art. The two great American artists in England at the end of the century — Abbey and Sargent — were also to make notable contributions. There was a third, one of the greatest of American painters living in London at the end of the century, James McNeill Whistler. This splendid draftsman and etcher was a true cosmopolitan. It would be hard to see any influence coming from him in the social relations of Great Britain and America. About Edwin Abbey's influence, however, there can be no doubt.

Edwin Austin Abbey was born in Philadelphia in 1852. He grew up determined to be an artist, and obtained employment from the publishing house of Harper in New York. In 1878 he sailed for England, to execute drawings on English life for this firm.

> Destiny plays us strange tricks. This young American's purpose in sailing for the old country was to do no more than gather enough English atmosphere to qualify him to complete an edition of Herrick and attack other kindred

themes with authority. He little thought that he was not only to make his home there, and live his life there, but to become the quintessential delineator of the England of the past. Yet so it was. This visitor from the New World was destined to do more towards the visible reconstruction of English life of the past than any other man.[1]

Abbey was in pictures what Washington Irving was in letters, the interpreter of Old England, especially of eighteenth-century England, not merely to the Americans, but to the English themselves. This son of Philadelphia had envisaged England before he arrived, found it already familiar on arrival, entered at once into the unbroken tradition of English life.

It was not wholly accidental that after the usual depressing experience, chronicled by so many Americans, of landing at Liverpool's dingy dock-quarter in dismal weather, Abbey should go straight on to Stratford-on-Avon, and put up at the Red Horse where Washington Irving had slept. The hotel reminded Abbey of Charles Dickens, the supreme portrayer of inn-life of the stage-coach days. Recklessly the young American artist, almost penniless, took a private room, *the* room of Irving, with a bright fire burning, which the artist could poke, as Irving did, and before which he could stretch his feet. It was a fine introduction to England for a young stranger who had such a zest for the Washington Irving period. Abbey was unable to pay the bill for the luxury of a private room in the inn, so he left his trunks behind him and went up to London with a debt to be worked off. He took a lodging in Montague

[1] E. V. Lucas, *Life and Work of E. A. Abbey* (1921), I, 60.

Place, and later another near the house where Benjamin West had lived in Newman Street. He sent his drawings over to Harper's, and fairly soon was not merely out of debt, but was able to send thirty-five dollars a week home to his father in Philadelphia.

Abbey came to London with introductions to the English artist, Fred Barnard, and the American artist, George Henry Boughton, already well-established in public estimation, and later elected R.A. Barnard and Boughton introduced Abbey to that wonderfully vivid Victorian artist-world. There, everybody seemed to know everyone, and all were kind, jolly, sociable, and full of knowledge of their art. Abbey heard Leighton explaining things with the greatest care, clearing up obscure questions; he listened to Whistler's epigrams, laughed at his conceit; visited Alma Tadema's wonderful 'Roman' house at St. John's Wood; met Browning, came to know Henry James, went to Paris with Frank Millet. His greatest friend was Alfred Parsons, one of the most sympathetic painters of the English countryside, and therefore a man particularly after Abbey's own heart. Soon caught up in a bewitching social life, in a round of formal and informal entertainments, enjoying to the full the generous company of brilliant men of art and letters, Abbey still hankered after the coterie of artists, the Tile Club, to which he had belonged, in New York. 'It seems to me,' he wrote in 1880, two years after arriving in England, 'that small, strong, earnest bodies of *live* men, working together and using each other's experience, as the Tile Club does, cannot help but become a strong power and influence for good. I never seemed to work so easily and surely as I did when I was with the boys on Long Island.' Abbey was ill when he wrote this, and felt depressed. As a matter of fact he had all the society he needed; he created social life as he went on his way, and gave and took, yet remained American and considered himself as representing American art. 'I am sure,' he wrote in 1880, 'that the coming ten years will place American art on an equal footing with that of any other country.' The prophecy was largely fulfilled.

These days or years — the eighties and nineties — were great days for art, at any rate in some respects if not in others. The British artists, in prosperous bourgeois London, Manchester, and Glasgow, had splendid markets. They had a thousand guineas for a picture, wore wonderful velvet jackets, and were, Abbey said, 'aggravatingly prosperous.' It was the time of fine illustration — the work of painters, etchers, and engravers — in the magazines of the general public. The United States editors had brought this kind of magazine to a high condition of perfection — the magazine of serious, dignified stories and articles, with a wealth of splendid illustration. *Harper's* and *Scribner's* and the *Century* circulated in Great Britain, taught Great Britain the art of magazine illustration and provided artists with a splendid medium for expression. Of these illustrators of the greatest days of the illustrated magazine, Abbey was king.

His art prospered. Fortune smiled. Abbey paid a visit to America, renewed his association with the Tile Club, saw his friends at Harper's. His work, however, was still in England, illustrating editions of Shakespeare's plays or Goldsmith's *She Stoops to Conquer*, and other literary masterpieces of Old England; and this work he did with inimitable grace and charm. He married, settled down in Bloomsbury, added friend to friend: William Black, George du Maurier, Austin Dobson. The Thames Valley and the Cotswold country lured him — the country of cool stone houses, quiet valleys, gentle streams. In 1890 the Abbeys bought an old house at Fairford called Morgan Hall. The clean little market-town, famous for the ancient stained glass of its church, on the edge of the Cotswolds, and in the flowery meadows of the Upper Thames, was the Abbeys' home for twenty years.

Morgan Hall was a place where Abbey could entertain his friends, paint, and play cricket. He became an enthusiast for cricket, and had a special week of it every year, in July, at Morgan Hall, on the lawn or a meadow by the house. William Morris, Alfred Parsons, Henry James, Sargent, visited him. The house was usually full of guests. During one cricket week, Henry James composed an oratorio every evening on the events of the day — at least Abbey declared that this was so in a letter to his brother.

In 1899 the Abbeys also took a London house, a pleasant, Old-World place with a paved court, called Chelsea Lodge, 42, Tite Street, near the houses where Whistler and Sargent lived. He was enormously in demand, for work both in America and in England. He helped in the work on the panels of the House of Lords. He made the paintings for the dome of the

Capitol of Pennsylvania at Harrisburg. He did the picture of the coronation of Edward VII at Westminster (where Abbey wore his Royal Academy uniform with sword). And by his wonderful series of illustrations he reinterpreted Shakespeare to the whole world. John Hay, United States Secretary of State, was one of his many correspondents. Abbey complained humorously to Hay about America's fiscal policy. He called himself 'one of the small class of expatriated American citizens who is taxed by his grateful country for sending his "things" home, instead of disposing of them here. I have sometimes wondered how it can be legal to discriminate against artists in this way. The members of other learned professions are let off.... If ever there was a learned profession ours is one, and one it takes a long time to learn too. I doubt if anyone ever got it "good and learned" — and, as a rule, the reason we stay here is because we are students, and not, as I have heard, because it is cheap (which I have yet to discover).' [1]

The turn of the century, or the years covered by the Spanish-American War and the Boer War, was the time of the great turn in British-American relations, always a little uneasy until that date. Hay was Ambassador in London during the early part of the Spanish-American War, and Secretary of State at Washington during the Boer War. Abbey wrote from London to Hay in December, 1899, when the Boer War was going badly for the British, and when Hay was finding matters of state a particular source of anxiety:

[1] E. V. Lucas, *op. cit.*, II, 340.

I saw the other day in a casual number of the New York *Herald* a portrait of yourself so sicklied over with lines and marks that I have meant ever since to write a word or two of sympathy. I have nothing much to say, save that we are very proud to know you, and that we wish there were more like you, and to send you all our best wishes for the new year and century. Here everything is pretty grey just now. All our friends have somebody at the front — and many more on the way. Now that the 'Yeomanry' have been called out, one wonders who will be left! One realises how much of one family England is.[1]

Five years later, Hay, who was on holiday at Nauheim, and an ill man in his last year, received a letter from Abbey:

It is extraordinary, when one looks over it, the amount you have accomplished in the last twenty years.... You have made a difference in the world's history since those days — and every American worthy of the name is glad you were born.

Hay replied:

Getting sick and dying is not nearly so serious a matter as it is to lose sight and touch of one's friends in the process. Your letter makes me ache to see you. By the same mail comes an invitation to Cambridge, to receive a degree the week after I sail for home. *That* is past praying for, but I hope to see you and Mrs. Abbey during the few hours we are to be in London.[2]

Hay actually did see Abbey in London on this last visit. In a sense, they were workers in the same field.

Abbey, who had a splendid historical sense, was keenly interested in Sir George Trevelyan's history of

[1] Lucas, *op. cit.*, II, 347.   [2] Lucas, *op. cit.*, II, 410.

the American Revolution, which he read, as fast as it came out, volume by volume, with 'deep emotion.' He found it helpful in stimulating his imagination for executing his Harrisburg pictures, which are surely the supreme interpretation of the American colonial period. The years passed away in happy, strenuous work. 'There are no holidays in my trade,' Abbey said. 'It is always in the back of one's head, no matter what one is doing.' He had his visits to America; he had hosts of friends there and in England. He enjoyed life everywhere, and describes it in his cheerful, crisp letters: Chapel at Trinity, Cambridge, where he heard four hundred undergraduates roar out a hymn: 'And I could not but think they might be given more than one hymn to roar. I also thought the effect of the whole thing would be enhanced if they washed their surplices oftener.' And: 'Assheton and I dined at Trinity — very well, I thought — the two high tables crammed.... We had much excellent port in the combination room, and home to bed rather merry by ten o'clock.' The motorcar — a 'noiseless Daimler' — made possible an even more nearly perfect knowledge of England. Henry James helped in the interpretation, as when he wrote, of a visit that he and the Abbeys made to Overstrand in Norfolk:

> Overstrand is a sort of miniature Norfolk Newport, with a group of people who see each other constantly all winter ... dining, tea-ing, lunching or chattering again with the utmost fury; but the Norfolk country all new to me, full of character and strength, and Norwich Cathedral a much finer thing than I had supposed. I was struck with the boundless *wealth* of everyone.

This is just how the Englishman feels who goes to the American Rhode Island Newport.

After a short illness, Abbey died at Chelsea in 1911. His great compeer, Sargent (like Abbey a tremendous worker), lived to 1925, and was able to give some service with his art in the World War. The two Americans, exercising their art in Chelsea and in the Cotswolds, had an influence, difficult of course to define, yet indubitable, on the public life of their countries, on the United States and on Great Britain. Neither Abbey nor Sargent was at all political; it was by reason of their long lives of fruitful work for two countries, of their large human sympathy, their great-heartedness, their genius for friendship, that, unconscious of themselves, their influence went forth.

In these halcyon years of the end of the nineteenth century and beginning of the early twentieth, the Americans in England seemed to be designed by nature for the maintenance of a high and graceful culture there, a humanism like that of the Renaissance, eager, fastidious, broad-minded, and sympathetic. Henry James, Abbey, and Sargent by themselves were sufficient to make the American contribution notable; and they were not alone: Frank Millet of Russell House, Broadway, the painter who was lost on the *Lusitania*; Edward Perry Warren of Oxford University and Lewes House (Sussex), a classical scholar and art-critic of distinction; others, who are still alive.

For the career of humanist the Americans in England had many advantages. They were, mostly, wealthy, or at any rate in comfortable circumstances. They came of good stock, and had been brought up in cultured, refined homes. They had received an excellent education, at schools and colleges of New England, at Oxford or Cambridge or on the Continent. They started with an artistic sensitiveness. Life in a society in which they had not been born, and which had a certain air of freshness for them, was intellectually and artistically stimulating. Leisurely and affluent, they could cultivate friendship and society, conversation and the play of wit and ideas, indispensable to high and humane culture. These men and women were the splendid fruit of two centuries of American education, transported to a European environment, and making it their own.

Their 'humanity' (in the Renaissance sense of the word) never made them lose their American quality; without that quality they could not have been what they were. They had the best of lives for those who can lead it, a life in two hemispheres, friendships on both sides of the ocean, the old and settled society of Europe, the society of the American city and country, partly new, partly developed from the European source.

James McNeill Whistler was one of the best known, most talked-of, most beloved, of Americans in London. He was born in 1834 at the great textile-manufacturing town of Lowell, Massachusetts. His father and many of his relatives were, or had been, soldiers. James or 'Jimmy' obtained a nomination from President Filmore to West Point in 1851. He was never a very serious cadet, but he was three years at West Point and learned something; but he did not proceed to an officer's commission.

In 1855 Whistler went to Paris to study art and lived the kind of life that George du Maurier (who was a friend of Whistler in the Latin Quarter) described so well in *Trilby*. Whistler came to know Thackeray and the author's talented family when they visited the Paris International Exhibition. Artists' life in the Latin Quarter was delightful to a born Bohemian and good fellow like Whistler, but it did not bring in much money; and once at least Jimmy is said to have pawned his coat. In 1859 he took up his residence in London.

Whistler soon had many friends in London. His sister was married to Sir Seymour Haden, a well-known surgeon and amateur of art. For a time he lived with the Hadens at 62, Sloane Street, Chelsea. The first picture which he exhibited at the Royal Academy was 'At the Piano,' 1860, a work which shows his genius for drawing, for colour, for light and shade; the sitter at the piano is Lady Haden. For some years he regularly exhibited at the Academy, but he was never elected an Academician, although under the liberal charter of George III, Americans are as eligible as anyone else, and a number have been elected.

Whistler, though very lovable, was inclined to be quarrelsome. So after a time he left the Hadens' house, and took up quarters with du Maurier in Newman Street. This partnership, too, only lasted a short time. In 1863 he set up house with his mother at what is now 101, Cheyne Walk, Chelsea, in the street where Thomas Carlyle lived. Whistler has left a touching portrait of his mother (he painted old people beautifully, such as Thomas Carlyle among others). Dante Gabriel Rossetti lived not far away in Tudor House. Whistler frequently went there in the evenings and met Burne-Jones, Swinburne, and Meredith. Both Rossetti and Whistler loved blue and white Japanese prints, though Rossetti could not paint their shades and colouring as Whistler did.

Suddenly and unaccountably, Whistler took ship from London with some adventurers left over from the American Civil War. They sailed to Valparaiso to help the Chileans in a war against Spain. Jimmy had a baptism of fire and said that he ran away like the rest, only faster. He came back to London with some beautiful pictures. 'Whistler was the first to paint the night.... Night, beautiful everywhere from Valparaiso to Venice, is never more beautiful than in London.' [1]

Finding his fortunes (as he thought) improving, Whistler had a house built for himself. Artists in those days did very well. Whether as painters of portraits, of Greek and Roman feasts and baths, of country-house gardens and gables, they never satiated the wealthy public. Picture after picture was sold for a large sum: and the flourishing artists built themselves ornate and stately mansions in St. John's Wood or Kensington. They were rich, and their art became a trifle commonplace. Whistler, however, was never commonplace; and he was never rich. He could not build a great mansion. Nevertheless he had fine ideas, and he insisted on the house being built just as he liked it. The result was the

[1] E. and J. Pennell, *The Life of Whistler* (1920).

'White House,' Tite Street, a charming house, but too dear for Whistler. It was built in 1878 and he had to sell it in 1879. The house and a libel action which he brought (and won with a farthing damages) against Ruskin made him bankrupt. Jimmy was not very careful about money. He was the soul of generosity, and entertained his friends incessantly, giving them the best of food and wine, in addition to his own inimitable conversation. His bills were rather large and ran on for a long time. One long-suffering greengrocer is said to have let an account for tomatoes mount up to £600. Jimmy evidently liked tomatoes, or his friends did. He gave breakfasts as well as dinners. Lord Houghton, the greatest of breakfast entertainers after Samuel Rogers, came to these morning feasts; but Whistler was no base imitator. He invented *Sunday breakfasts*.

Although probably never in easy financial circumstances, Whistler managed to keep his head above water in later life, and to have, and to give, a good time. He had a house (not the one which he had built and sold) at 13, Tite Street. His pictures came into great request. He lectured too, for Mr. D'Oyly Carte, at Prince's Hall, on Art, at ten o'clock in the evening. The 'Ten O'clock' was a famous event. At the end of his life he lived at 74, Cheyne Walk, the same street in which he had started his rather battered but happy household life forty years before. Although apparently a confirmed bachelor, he had married a widow in 1888; but his wife died in 1896. Whistler died in 1903 at his house in Cheyne Walk.

People who did not know John Singer Sargent doubted if he was an American, but none of his friends did. A great artist, drawing freely on the classical tradition of Europe, working with the best masters, associating with the high artists of his age, is necessarily a citizen of the world; his appeal is to the whole world. The Americans who live in Europe would not stay there if they were aggressive and assertive; they live there, as at other times they live in America, because their culture is humane; it transcends political frontiers. Sargent's physical life was, indeed, less American than that of most. He was born in Florence; he was educated there and in other Italian cities, or in Paris. He fixed his home in London. This was the place that suited his genius; therefore he naturally chose it. Yet he crossed the Atlantic, westbound, some thirteen times, for long periods of residence, and did much of his work in studios in New York and Boston. Nevertheless, his home, so far as he had one, was in 31, Tite Street, Chelsea. There he had his fixed studio, his pictures, furniture, books, manservant and maidservant, but he usually stayed there only for the London season.

The places he stayed in were particularly beautiful: Broadway in the Cotswolds, Fairford in the Thames Valley, Pershore in Worcestershire. He went abroad, of course, to France, Italy, Spain, Austria. It was a long and singularly happy life, of creative art, sustained industry, cheerful companionship, literature. He died in the middle of the night, a volume of Voltaire at his bedside. All England and America that could do so ordered portraits; and he painted sincerely, carefully,

JOHN SINGER SARGENT

with a gift of original interpretation which his clients sometimes thought rather terrible. He painted the heroic tragedy of the British soldier of the World War in 'Gassed'; the panel in the Widener Library at Harvard pictures for ever the Young American Army on its eager way to the great struggle in Europe.

In the Tate Gallery of London the Sargent Room enshrines England's public collection of the master. An entire gallery or hall is given over to Sargent. After passing through galleries filled with the quaint and graceful pictures of the Pre-Raphaelite School, glorious landscapes of Turner, and the always interesting and frequently beautiful pictures of the modern French school, you go through into the Sargent collection. The first picture is 'Carnation, lily, lily, rose,' the loveliest of all pictures of garden-flowers and children. The rest, except for one or two copies after Old Masters (El Greco, Velasquez), a Venetian interior, and Claude Monet in a wood-scene, are portraits; nine pictures of the Wertheimer family; the Earl of Wemyss (who is said to have disliked the portrait); the much-discussed portrait of Madame Gautreau, a work of Sargent's early Paris years; the hunting peer with the intellectual features, Lord Ribblesdale; Thomas Hardy, not looking very distinguished; Professor Ingram Bywater, whose edition of Aristotle's *Ethics* the clever classical undergraduates at Oxford used always to have to read; Ellen Terry, acting. It was a unique honour for pictures to be hung in the National Gallery while their painter was still alive; but this is surely nothing compared to the honour of having a whole gallery to oneself in the great national collection of modern schools. The tranquil Sargent took his honours as they came almost without comment. His friends loved him; to the general public he was rather inscrutable. Yet few artists have given more pleasure to their generation, or had a more wholesome influence; none have reacted more sanely to their environment.

When Sargent died in 1925, all Europe and America recognised the passing of a great artist. He has enriched the world with works of rare beauty and originality. Although seldom seen in public, known by sight to comparatively few, he was a familiar name, and even a familiar, if somewhat elusive, personality to two continents. The charm of his character appears naturally in his works: single-minded devotion to his art; entire sincerity and honesty of vision, sympathy with every type and character, a serene outlook on life. More universal in his tastes than Henry James, Sargent nevertheless had the same severe standards, the same humorous quality, the same wise vision upon a world of living and thinking people. It is the quintessence of the old American culture, which saw no barrier in sea or frontier.

XIV

THE FRINGES OF DIPLOMACY

PROFESSIONAL diplomatists, the 'diplomatists of career,'
live in countries not altogether of their own choosing;
and their social relations may be regarded, to some
extent, as part of their business. There have been,
however, American diplomatists who knew England by
living in it long before they joined the career. Henry
White was one of them. 'The relationships he formed
supplemented and strengthened his diplomatic work,
and, as with a number of representatives from the time
of Benjamin Franklin, gave his official activities an
invaluable background.'[1] He first visited England
when he was eight years old, and for the second time
when he was fifteen. On this visit the White family
lived for two or three months in 'the placid mid-
Victorian world of Thackeray,' in Cavendish Square,
London. Later White wrote:

> We frequently walked past Apsley House which was
> presented by the British nation to the Duke of Welling-
> ton, and at which in after years during my long connec-

[1] Nevins, *Henry White* (1930), 3.

tion with our legation (and subsequent embassy) I was to be an occasional guest of the third duke and his wife. It is not improbable that the realisation that the history of England and our own were the same up to 1776, and that there was far more in common between the two countries than between America and any other, was then implanted in my mind.

In 1870 the White household was again in England. They belonged to an old-established Baltimore family. Much of Henry's youth had been passed at Hampton, his grandfather Ridgely's Maryland estate. Country-house life was therefore familiar to him, and he took to it readily in England. The White family had considerable resources. Henry was able to rent a hunting-box at Market Harborough in Leicestershire, and to hunt for nine successive winters with famous packs, the Belvoir, the Quorn, the Pytchley, the Cottesmore. 'The hunting-field,' he wrote, 'is a wonderful place of training for character, good manners, good temper, and coolness of judgment' — obviously not a bad school, at any rate for part of his time, for a diplomatist. He visited at neighbouring country-houses — Althorpe, Rockingham Castle, Cottesbrooke, Burley. He had two Baltimore friends at St. John's College, Oxford, and through them came to know and appreciate 'the interesting talk in the common-rooms of the colleges after dinner, the beautiful services in the college chapels, the boating on the Isis, the semi-monastic character of residence in the old rooms of the colleges.' In 1879 he married Miss Margaret Rutherford, who belonged to a well-known New York family. In 1883 Secretary of

State Frelinghuysen appointed him Secretary of Legation in Vienna where Alphonso Tuft was American
Minister; and in 1884 he joined the London Legation
under James Russell Lowell.

James G. Blaine, Secretary of State at Washington
before Frelinghuysen, had warned White to guard
against taking on the airs of an Englishman and becoming practically not an American. The envious or
the critics sometimes hinted at some such result in
Henry White, but history discerns in him only the
career-diplomatist, serving his country and the cause
of peace. The Administration at Washington in a
diplomatic crisis was very glad to make use of his good
sense and adaptability, of his familiarity with English
politics and society.

The Whites took a house in Hertford Street, later in
Grosvenor Street, number 9. He had a genial, frank,
natural manner, quietly sympathetic. He belonged
to rather exclusive clubs — the Knickerbocker in New
York, the Marlborough, the Bachelors', the St. James's,
in London. He also had a small country-house, Rams-
lade, in Berkshire. Soon, he and his wife belonged to
a social group which took itself seriously and was
certainly brilliant, but which perhaps has received as
much attention as it deserves.

High society, even when it is brilliant and clever,
always seems, at any rate to those who are outside and
possibly to those who are within, to be somewhat out
of touch with reality. Its influence upon public affairs,
although never wholly insignificant, is often overestimated. The 'Souls,' as the famous group was

called, consisted of a group of socially well-connected young people, of a rather daring turn of mind, all possessed with a profound admiration of each other's brilliance; justifiably, too, for a very large number of them rose to great celebrity. The circle had 'wealth, beauty, intellect, culture,' also ambition and political influence. Two of them became Prime Ministers, Balfour and Asquith; one became Lord Chancellor, Haldane; one, Viceroy of India and Secretary of State for Foreign Affairs, Curzon; one, Secretary of State for the Colonies, Alfred Lyttelton; one (or two, counting Haldane), Secretary of State for War; one, George Wyndham, Chief Secretary for Ireland. Asquith and Haldane did not consider themselves members of the 'Souls,' though it is hard to know what membership meant; they were certainly familiar with all the group. It flourished in the daring nineties, when *The Yellow Book* was being published, and Aubrey Beardsley's drawings had a certain vogue. The 'Souls' played tennis and boated, talked literature, philosophy, and religion. They lived their week-ends in great country-houses: Wilton, Taplow Court, Panshanger, Ashridge, Studley Royal, Stanway, Mells. The group was fairly catholic in its tastes, provided that a man had genius or talent. 'I must say I am disposed to draw the line at Oscar Wilde,' Henry White wrote to his wife. White and his beautiful wife lived the social life of the 'Souls,' but they had more distinctly literary associations in friendship with George Meredith and Henry James.

About the year 1893 the 'Souls' as a group broke up. Curzon was off on a journey round the world.

White was on a visit to the United States, and owing to a change in the Administration at Washington was dismissed from the American diplomatic service. He had done good work in England; 'his knowledge of English life and affairs was of far-reaching advantage to him in all his diplomatic contacts. It was not, unfortunately, an unmixed advantage, for by the completeness of his identification with English circles he seemed to some of his countrymen to lose that rigid Americanism which they thought essential to an ambassador in London, and thus raised up an impediment to his own promotion.' [1] In 1897, however, he returned to London as Secretary of Embassy to John Hay.

The eminently sociable John Hay knew England well, having made frequent and long visits to Europe in his leisurely, ample way of life. The short period of his ambassadorship, about eighteen months, is notable for the alteration which all observers noticed in the mutual attitudes of America and England. The number of Americans who visited England had increased greatly since the early eighties when the big movement from America to England set in. John Hay, Henry Adams, Chauncey Depew, Joseph Choate, Senator Hoar, might almost be called well-known figures in London in the nineties; and there were the permanent or semi-permanent American residents like Henry James, Sargent, Abbey, Millet. 'A new and brighter era was dawning in Anglo-American relations.' John Hay thought that the United States, if it gave the slightest encouragement, could have the alliance of Great Britain. The Americans who knew England well

[1] Nevins, *op. cit.*, 54.

had no difficulty in understanding the cordiality of the British Government and British public. In Washington, however, wrote Henry White (on a visit there in 1898): 'They all seem surprised to find (except perhaps Lodge) that the feeling which we have always known exists in England, really does so, and having ascertained this to be the case, they are tremendously appreciative of it.' The United States was engaged in the Spanish War, was distinctly unpopular on the Continent of Europe, and responded all the more warmly to the unexpected sympathy of England.

The twentieth century thus opened with the best of prospects in Anglo-American relationships. Ambassadors came (Joseph H. Choate, 1899–1905; Whitelaw Reid, 1905–12) who were eminent social figures as well as important diplomatists. Whitelaw Reid was a particularly striking example of the American in England, for he took the gorgeous Park Lane mansion called Dorchester House (now demolished), and had a palatial country-seat, Wrest Park in Bedfordshire. Theodore Roosevelt, after his term as President, visited England in 1910 and stayed for three weeks at Dorchester House. He made a great impression on London, and on Oxford University, where he gave the Romanes Lecture and declared his views on the writing of history to the assembled professors and tutors. Roosevelt's visit might almost be called a great unofficial embassy, for he made statements on public affairs which were much appreciated in Great Britain. Rudyard Kipling wrote to Brander Matthews:[1] 'Roosevelt has come

[1] Bishop, *Theodore Roosevelt and his Time* (1920), II, 258–59; cf. G. M. Trevelyan, *Sir George Otto Trevelyan, A Memoir* (1932), 143–44.

and gone and done our state great service. Here you have one single-minded person, saying and doing quite casually things which ought to set the world planning; instead of which the world says: "Thank you! Please do it again."'

With the coming of Walter Hines Page to the London Embassy, the United States found its ideal representative. He was only by accident in diplomacy, and made no mark in it until the World War came, and discovered his passionate genius. In his year and a half before the war he was the observant visitor settling down in an ancient and ordered society in which he felt all the kinship of history, culture, and race.

Page approached England obviously with great zest. On his way over, on the *Baltic* he wrote:

> There are three titled Englishmen who sit at the table with me on this ship — one a former Lord Mayor of London, another a peer, and the third an M.P. Damn their self-sufficiencies! They do excite my envy. *They* don't shoulder the work of the world; they shoulder the world and leave the work to be done by somebody else. Three days' stories and political discussion with them have made me wonder why the devil I've been so industrious all my life. They know more than I know; they are richer than I am; they have been about the world more than I have; they are far more influential than I am; and yet one of them asked me today if George Washington was a born American! I said to him, 'Where the devil do you suppose he came from — Hades?' And he laughed at himself as heartily as the rest of us laughed at him and didn't care a hang![1]

[1] Hendrick, *The Life and Letters of W. H. Page* (ed. 1924), 130.

When Page arrived in London, he noticed that politics were dividing high society. Social relations were suspended between Conservative and Liberal hostesses. The introduction into Parliament by the Liberal Administration of a Home Rule Bill and a Parliament Bill (to restrict the powers of the House of Lords) had not merely increased the division between political parties, but had bitterly estranged people in social life. Page had to be very careful whom he and Mrs. Page invited to their dinner-parties, for he heard that some men would not shake hands with each other, and that their wives felt equally embittered, and that if one came into a room the others would walk out.

It is quite true that the Liberal Administration of 1906–14, brilliant but uncompromising, had created or provoked more bitterness in politics than had ever existed before, even in the fiercest times of the early eighteenth-century Whigs and Tories. The social cleavage resulting from political estrangement was, however, not a new thing. Henry White noticed it in the eighteen-nineties, as the result of Mr. Gladstone's first and second Home Rule Bills; the 'Souls' had to be careful of their social contacts when Liberals came near their circle, although they themselves did not all belong to the same party.

Page obviously came to England prepared to like the English. When a man approaches any country and people in this frame of mind, he is never disappointed. It has sometimes been said that the ambassadors of the United States to England are at a disadvantage as compared with the English ambassadors to the United

States, owing to their lack of diplomatic training, and owing to the seductiveness of London social life. As a matter of fact, however, it is very doubtful if this criticism of American diplomacy is justified. In Washington (as Henry James remarked) there is the most entertaining society in America; high life in the Federal Capital is as seductive as life in London, and in some ways (because politicians and diplomatists all live close together there) exercises a more compelling influence. The records of American diplomacy can be searched from the days of John Adams, John Jay, and Richard Rush to the opening of the Great War, and no incident is to be found in which American diplomatists in any way forgot their country's interest or ceased persistently to sustain it. That they all liked London life, except perhaps John Adams, is undeniable.

It was a new world that Page suddenly entered, in the early summer of the year 1913. He had never been in England before; on the other hand, it was not absolutely strange to him, owing to his education and his knowledge of men. The London season was in full swing when he arrived, and naturally he at once received many invitations. The first reception to which he went was at the house of some duchess. The powdered footmen were the chief novelty that impressed him; and perhaps also the fact that he was not introduced to anybody, except for the bare announcement of his name by the butler on entering the drawing-room. At dinner-parties introductions were made, but in so slurred a voice that it was scarcely intelligible. All this London life was rather breathless. Page and his wife were invited to twice as many luncheons and dinners as they could attend. He went to all he could. At each 'a sea of friendly faces' greeted him. In his brilliant letters describing this social round of entertainments, he persists in his assertion that he was never introduced to anybody, or when he was, that he could not grasp the name. Somebody would say, 'Uh — o — oh — Lord Xz ww x k mpt.'

Judging by the number of dukes and duchesses and other peers and peeresses mentioned in Page's letters, one can be certain that he took a very real and lively, though naïve and innocent, pleasure in high life and its feudal and romantic attributes. It was indeed a very fine aristocracy, very rich, yet (as Henry White had also found) relatively simple in its way of life, patriotic but tolerant, domesticated and respectable, like the Royal Court which set the standard. They were, as Page said, all very nice people, courteous and limitlessly hospitable. Page said that they had more courtesy and made far shorter speeches than Americans. The servants, too, had special virtues. It is true that they had too much of the servant mentality for Page to admire them completely; but they were very good servants. The Pages kept fifteen servants in the house at 6, Grosvenor Square. They did much the same things as seven good servants would do in the United States, but did them much better. If a dinner-party for twenty-four people was to be given, Mrs. Page simply gave the butler a list of their names, and after that needed to take no more interest in the matter. The dinner would be perfectly cooked and served, and all the guests properly announced. When the evening was finishing, the butler would see all the guests politely out of the front door and show them to their carriages. The butler's wages were about as high as 'the ramshackle nigger' that Page employed to look after his house at Garden City, Long Island. All the same the whole household and life at Grosvenor Square cost Page a good deal. Nobody, he said, would extract the secret from him. He was having his great chance in life, and he seized it with both hands, and did not care if he spent his whole fortune.

The atmosphere was not merely charged with courtesy, but with friendliness and cordiality. The English and the Americans, in spite of the facts of international law, persist in not regarding each other as foreigners. Henry Adams slipped into this way of thought in London, and spoke of Americans and foreigners as well-defined, separate groups. Page was interested, too, in looking into a club book to find members classified as British, Colonial, American, and Foreign. Page himself had often tried in a dining-room by looking at the guests to make out who was English and who American, and had failed, and everybody else failed who tried, until they began to talk. Even talking is not quite a safe test.

The habit of entertaining at breakfast, about nine o'clock or later, still went on. Henry Adams had gone to Lord Houghton's breakfasts in the sixties, and met Goldwin Smith, Leslie Stephen, Tennyson, and many other famous men. White had gone to Sir George Trevelyan's breakfasts in the nineties. Mr. Lloyd

George gave breakfasts in the year before the war. They were political, naturally, not literary, but they continued the tradition.

Like many other Americans who have lived in England and observed it, like Henry Adams, for instance, and Henry James, Page was interested in considering whether the English were declining, whether the days of their greatness were over. He came quickly to the conclusion that they were not. He believed that in politics and in political morality they had made great advances since the time of rotten boroughs; and he was of opinion that they played cricket, and governed and fought better than they had ever done. He admired their public men. There was in those days, and had been for about sixty years, a particular type of public servant. Charles Eliot Norton described two of them, of the last quarter of the nineteenth century. Hugh Childers, who was Secretary of State for War in 1880 and Home Secretary in 1886, he called 'one of the solid, strong, well-mannered, quiet, genial Englishmen.' Fitz-james Stephen, who was a judge of the High Court, he called 'an excellent specimen of the men to whom England chiefly owes her greatness — men of solid, sincere intelligence, of vast capacity for work, of large frame and brain, eminently healthy, four-square and even with the world.' Page had a similar admiration for Morley and Grey.

The Englishman, Page thought, had always tended to be afraid of the future; it was this that kept him so alert. He agreed with Henry James who complained of the small amount of conversation that was really worth

WALTER H. PAGE

listening to, but he would not go so far as to say that
the English were dull — 'not dull, so much as steady.'
What most contributed to give them their vast power
in the world was their capital — and they were spending
their capital. For this reason, the leaderships of the
world would pass to the United States; 'the great
economic tide of the century flows our way,' wrote the
American.

If the world-influence of the Anglo-Saxons was
passing from England to the United States, it would be
well for the English to recognise community of interest
with America. They were ready enough to do so; indeed they had — at least the whole 'governing class'
of England had — 'an exaggerated admiration for
the American people'; but they lacked respect for the
American Government. Ignorance, 'unfathomable ignorance,' was the cause of this. 'If the Town Treasurer
of Yuba Dam gets a $100 "rake off" on a paving
contract, our city government is a failure.' The American newspapers were partly the cause of such ignorance
and misconception. The 'Yellow Press' made a mis-
leading impression, and American correspondents of
English newspapers sent 'exactly the wrong news' from
New York or Chicago or Washington to London.
People in political and high social circles took a lively
interest in American affairs. Mr. Wilson gradually
impressed his strong personality upon them. At first
the English showed only a 'mild curiosity' in him; but
soon they were eagerly asking questions. 'Tell me
something about your great President,' was the promis-
ing remark of a lady to whom Page sat next at dinner

in the early period of his ambassadorship. The ignorance of the two countries, 'each of the other,' was
'beyond belief,' although the best book about America,
Bryce's *American Commonwealth*, was the work of an
Englishman.

Court life, like the conditions in the rest of high
society where Page moved and enjoyed himself so much,
was splendid yet simple. The dinner and the music
and the plate were all magnificent, 'but there is a human
touch about it that seems almost democratic.' The
King of Denmark, 'a country with fewer people and less
wealth than New Jersey,' came on a visit to his royal
relatives of England and contributed to the simple
family atmosphere of King George's circle. The uses
of the Crown were well understood. The King in
England is by statute a member of the established
Church of England, but the Scots have their established
Church too, and 'when the King comes to Scotland, by
Jehoshaphat! he is obliged to become a Presbyterian.'

These were rather highly charged times in the twelve
months before the war. Henry White in the early
nineties, after having experienced 'the brighter, gayer
side of European life' in the cosmopolitan society of
Paris, took pleasure in becoming acquainted through
London society with the most distinguished side of the
English nation, 'where men worked hardest and their
interests were broadest.'[1] Page's view of high society
in London led him to a somewhat similar conclusion.
'The really alert people are the aristocracy,' wrote Page
in the summer of 1914. He exaggerated the late hours

[1] Nevins, *Henry White*, 24.

of highly placed people. 'Nobody is in the Government offices, except clerks and secretaries, till the afternoon.' There was too much talk about war. 'Germany' was in everybody's mouth. 'They talk all the time of the danger and probability of war; they don't expect it; but most wars have come without warning, and they are all the time prepared to begin a fight in an hour.' Page did not think that this was a bellicose or provocative attitude; but it seems to indicate that Colonel House's remark, after his visit to Berlin in May, 1914 — 'it is militarism run mad' — was to some extent meant as a criticism of other nations as well as the Germans. There was in England, and perhaps in Germany and France, pessimism rather than militarism, an attitude of hopelessness in the face of the continual possibility or imminence of war — 'alas! I see a settled melancholy in most of their statesmanship and in more of their literature.' Resignation in face of the potential war-plague is not the way to avert its arrival.

Yet two things this island has of eternal value, its gardens and its men. 'You and I,' Page writes to Mr. Wilson, 'can never be thankful enough that our ancestors came of this stock.' The English, he says, 'have abundant wit, though less humour than the Americans. They have no coffee fit to drink and only three vegetables, two of these being cabbage. Yet they have the high art of living; they are a great people, and I like them.'

XV

COLLEGE PRESIDENTS AND
COLLEGE PROFESSORS

THE especial charm of English scenery lies, or lay, in its restful quality, the result of what Mr. Trevelyan, in his description of England in the age of Anne, has called 'the perfect balance between man and nature.' Probably all observers have noticed this; many in their various ways have tried to express it: Pastor Moritz, the kindly, late eighteenth-century German visitor; André Siegfried, the acute twentieth-century French observer; the British poets, who interpret their countrymen's view:

> How often have I paused on every charm,
> The sheltered cot, the cultivated farm,
> The never-failing brook, the busy mill,
> The decent church that topped the neighbouring hill.

The scenery of America has never attained this perfect balance between man and nature, except in a few old and settled parts where material progress has stopped, as in the New England countryside. In England, in spite of the increase in population, the balance was maintained throughout the eighteenth and nineteenth centuries. The 'Industrial Revolution' concentrated its efforts in the large towns. Man continued in the countryside, through a traditional and orderly development, to live harmoniously with nature; there were no harsh notes, and the rhythm of rural life was unbroken.

This was just the country for tired people, or for men of sensitive feeling to whom a tranquil environment was more congenial than grand, exciting scenes.

> Sky, mountains, rivers, winds, lake, lightnings! ye!
> With night, and clouds, and thunder, and a soul
> To make these felt and feeling, well may be
> Things that have made me watchful; the far roll
> Of your departing voices is the knell
> Of what in me is sleepless — if I rest.
> But where of ye, oh, tempests! is the goal?
> Are ye like those within the human breast?
> Or do ye find, at length, like eagles some high nest?

The Americans were not averse from visiting in Switzerland, nor indeed in any of the Continental countries; but on the whole England made the strongest appeal to them, for besides its particular charm of scenery, it had memories of homeland, and literary associations; it contained friends; its language was both a spiritual bond to Americans and an unconstrained means of communication. English literature is especially, perhaps uniquely, associated with particular places or districts: Stratford, Fleet Street, the Lakes. The cultured Americans 'knew their Lake District' better than most Englishmen.

Mr. Wilson in those years — on the whole happy, though marred by times of exhaustion and collapse — before he became Governor of New Jersey and President of the United States, was a man who turned to English country for relief. His father, who was a Presbyterian minister of Scottish descent, had brought him up to a life of walking, reading, and thinking. The things they read and talked over were largely drawn from English sources — Burke's *Speeches* and Adam Smith's *Wealth of Nations*, Bagehot's *English Constitution*, Green's *History of the English People* (which, Wilson maintained, was also a history of the American people), Wordsworth's poems, the *Edinburgh Review*. All this was, naturally, just part of his education, part of a large training in knowledge of his own country's history and institutions, as well as in the Greek and Latin culture and in German philosophy: the equipment of a great teacher of history and political science. Wilson was undoubtedly a great teacher. At Bryn Mawr, at Middletown, at Princeton, his students felt that they were associated with a man of strong mind, who had something definite and original to say, and who had a thorough method. The general public soon became aware of his remarkable qualities, and beset him with invitations (which he always accepted if free to do so) to lecture in every part of the country. When not lecturing to classes, or discussing with students, this active teacher and thinker with the 'single-track mind' was writing serious articles for the reviews and books for the learned press. He was a kind, if rather lonely, man (although he had friends). He usually took his walks alone, and (a bad habit!) spent them in thinking out subjects for lectures or essays. While a professor, he seems always to have had young relatives in his house, and with a small income was helping to 'see them through college,' while he incessantly wrote and lectured, stoked the furnace and helped in the household duties. It is small wonder that the tense bow-string sometimes seemed to snap. He had never been strong. As a young man his studies had at times been for months interrupted, when he would just carry on a broken, desultory reading, and wander rather aimlessly along the Delaware and among the docks at Wilmington. Though he had long ago thrown off this physical listlessness, and had found the cure in continual occupation in wholesome work, there were times when the springs of energy seemed suddenly to go dry, and Wilson collapsed. These times were what his biographer calls Wilson's nervous breakdowns; and so indeed they were, but not like those of ordinary men. When Wilson had a nervous breakdown, he did not become alarmed or stop his work — he only changed the rhythm. If it was not already near the vacation, he obtained leave of absence from his college, and went off — alone, because he could not afford to take his wife and daughters. He might go on a voyage to the West Indies, if time were short; the regular life on the ship, the good air and the good food, conduced to quiet thought and to the writing of books and lectures — for Wilson never really stopped working. If time permitted, he would take ship to England, and on arriving at Liverpool he would buy a bicycle; and on this 'wheel' he went through England, much of Scotland, and part of Ireland.

Wilson, the stern philosopher, the uncompromising college president, the powerful, practical statesman, is not, as portrayed by historians, a figure usually associated with poetry. Yet he loved particularly Wordsworth, Keats, Shelley, and Burns; he knew and appreciated Tennyson's poetry. Shakespeare, on the other hand, does not seem to have formed part of his vision of England. Wilson does not quote Shakespeare in his English journeys; and though he can scarcely have failed to visit Stratford when he bicycled to Warwick in 1896, there is no reference to it in the published letters and diaries.[1] Nor did he go much to the Continent of Europe. It was the Wordsworth country that drew him most. 'He became so enamoured of the Lake country that all of his subsequent visits to Europe, with the exception of a single short trip with Mrs. Wilson to France and Italy in 1903, drew him back irresistibly to Rydal and Keswick and Grasmere.'[2]

The Englishman who has read deeply in American sources, and the American who has read deeply in English, always find what they expect to find. Wilson went to make certain 'pious pilgrimages' in the England that he already knew: visits to Adam Smith's grave at Edinburgh, to Wordsworth's home in the Lakes, Burke's at Beaconsfield, Bagehot's in Somersetshire, Burns's in Dumfrieshire. He bicycled most of the way: thirty-three miles one day, seventeen another, without any hard-and-fast programme. He was not quite alone on this first visit, in 1896. He had

[1] R. S. Baker, *Woodrow Wilson, Life and Letters* (1928), II, 75–97.
[2] *Ibid.*, II, 76.

met a country lawyer and his wife in the ship coming over, Mr. and Mrs. C. A. Woods of South Carolina. They were kind, quiet people; and Wilson who was suffering from a sort of nervous collapse, found them ideal companions. They bicycled through the south of Scotland and Perthshire together. Wilson never concealed his ambition to be a statesman, though there seemed little enough likelihood of its being fulfilled. When Mr. Woods and he ultimately said good-bye, it was on the understanding that when the college professor became President of the United States, the country lawyer should be made a judge. The thing happened, and Wilson appointed Mr. Woods.

Travelling on a 'wheel' was more economical than the present-day method, and probably better for the health of an overworn, nervous man like Wilson. 'It is astonishing with how little fatigue the thing can be done on these roads,' he wrote to his wife; 'and it is quite as exhilarating and entertaining as I expected. The sweet, quiet country, the hawthorn hedge-rows, the quaint roadside villages, the great gates of estates with their pretty lodges, the good-natured, friendly people... all combine to make a great overmastering charm which itself makes the wheel run easily and with zest, as if to hurry from beauty to beauty.'[1]

Sometimes, as other athletes have been known to do, Wilson unostentatiously put his wheel into a train, and travelled for half a day in a third-class carriage; but he left the train at the right moment, for instance at Keswick, 'and rode on my wheel the sixteen enchanting

[1] R. S. Baker, II, 79.

miles to this place (Ambleside), by Thirlmere, Grasmere, and Rydal Water.' The enchanting miles drew
him to go back over the same road — to see Hartley
Coleridge's 'Nab Cottage,' the summer home of Dr.
Arnold of Rugby at Fox How, Wordsworth's grave at
Grasmere. 'One who knew nothing of the memories
and the poems associated with these places might well
bless the fortune that brought him to a region so complete, so various, so romantic, so irresistible in its
beauty — where the very houses seem suggested by
Nature and built to add to her charm.' [1]

From the Lake District, Wilson went to Warwick, to
the Woolpack Hotel, 'a quaint inn at the heart of the
Shakespeare country... this inexpressibly beautiful region, where England is to be seen looking as I had
dreamed it would look, and where memories crowd and
haunt so as to fill the mind and heart to overflowing.'
In Buckinghamshire memories came crowding even
more powerfully; memories of Burke, whose tomb he
found, but not Burke's house, for 'Gregories' is no
longer standing. The local people seemed scarcely to
have heard of Burke. Wilson looked for the origin of
the Washingtons, but found no 'distinct traces.' As
a matter of fact, he was off the proper track. The
Washingtons came from Sulgrave in Northampton-
shire.

The tracks of Wordsworth could be followed in other
places besides the Lake District. Wilson went off to the
West Country. For years he had treasured a small
volume of Wordsworth, a pocket-volume, but as any

[1] R. S. Baker, II, 80.

traveller can easily understand, he had somehow left it behind him in Princeton. He saw another copy, however, at Tewkesbury, in an old book-shop and bought it for a shilling. He was now travelling alone, and feeling strong, doing nearly twenty miles a day on the 'wheel.' There is a bridge over the Severn at Tewkesbury, so Wilson went onward into Monmouthshire and then down the Wye to Tintern Abbey which had inspired Wordsworth's 'Lines.' Wilson rode for nearly twenty miles along the valley of the Wye. 'Of all the parts of England I have seen, it has most won my heart,' he writes. 'It is so glad a stream and has such a secluded path amongst the hills that seem made for its setting.' *Secluded path* was perhaps not quite the right name for the road along the Wye which, even in the days before motor-cars, was a regular metalled driving-road. Probably in Wordsworth's time it really was almost a secluded path. Wilson sat on the grassy bank, read the whole poem (*Lines Composed a Few Miles above Tintern Abbey*), 'and was filled with an exalted emotion,' which he believed to be unforgettable. Changing the 'haves' into 'shall,' to suit a reader on his first visit to the Wye, Wilson repeated the lines:

> How oft —
> In darkness, and amid the many shapes
> Of joyless daylight; when the fretful stir
> Unprofitable, and the fever of the world,
> Shall hang upon the beatings of my heart,
> How oft, in spirit, shall I turn to thee,
> O sylvan Wye!

From Tintern there is a fine stretch of country, part
of Gloucestershire, all the way to Bristol. There the
'Bath' or 'Bristol' Avon is crossed, and the traveller
enters Somerset. This is steep, hilly country, although
the hills are scarcely above a thousand feet high. Wilson rode over those back-breaking roads, over the Men-
dip Hills, to Wells which he calls 'the heart of Somerset... lying in a sort of golden mist with its exquisite
cathedral, like a jewel in the midst.' [1]

Amid so many thrilling and attractive scenes, with
the harmonious setting of man and nature, and the
air of ancient peace, Wilson lost his heart to one place
after another. 'Wells won my heart above all,' he
wrote to his wife — 'not because it is a more perfect
jewel than the others, but because its perfect setting
(almost all the ancient ecclesiastical buildings grouped
about it unruined, and the quiet town keeping silence
about it) make it seem greater and more admirable.'
Glastonbury had a keen appeal for him too, being
'King Arthur's Isle of Avalon,'

> Where falls not hail, nor rain, nor any snow,
> Nor ever wind blows loudly, but it lies
> Deep meadowed, happy, fair with orchard lawns,
> And bowery meadows, crowned with summer sun.

There was, however, 'decay and melancholy ruin' at
Glastonbury; but Wells seemed to retain its antiquity
alive.[2]

Not merely Wells or Glastonbury, places which he
already knew by reputation, enchanted Wilson, but

[1] R. S. Baker, II, 84.   [2] R. S. Baker, II, 85.

the whole West Country. He discovered it; 'every turn of my ride brings me to things that interest me — to some outlook upon a beautiful countryside, to some village all character and age, a beautiful church standing in its quiet yard, in the midst, more noble in its proportions than most of our city churches, more lovingly finished in detail, though less ornate, an ancient monument of labour and of faith, conceived with a touch of majesty, and yet not too great for its secluded and rural seat — only the village church; or some bright busy town, I never knew anything about, but now find worth seeing, with monuments and noble or curious buildings of its own, old and new.' Such a place was Taunton, rich in historic memories and ancient buildings. The enchantment of it, however, was nothing to that of Clovelly. The effect was magical. 'I can only suppose that Clovelly bewitched me,' was his explanation. He felt as if he was walking in a picture or through a piece of stage-scenery, 'a sort of devised street built at a cunningly constructed world's fair.' The village is just a single precipitous street which cleaves the cliff, and is too steep for carriages, and quite as steep as foot-passengers like it to be. At the inn, they put Wilson all by himself in a tiny house (everything is on a small scale in Clovelly). In order to reach his room he had 'to climb through a little wonderfully tilted garden' behind the inn. The little house was on the topmost terrace, and contained nothing but the room and a half-cellar opening onto the terrace below. At one end of the room was a bay-window, 'as wide as our hall-way oriel [at Princeton University].' The dressing-table stood in the bay of the window. Wilson sat at the table, writing a letter home, and looking out over the sea, 'between the cliff-shoulders of the narrow place — below, the steep town, and the boats dancing in the tiny roadstead.' Wilson caught himself 'laughing aloud' with sheer joy in the quaint little room. He went down the steep street to the jetty, and sat looking at the fishing-boats and the sea, and dreaming 'of the place, of the sea, of you.'[1]

It might be thought that with a heart so overfull it would be impossible to hold more; nevertheless Oxford and Cambridge seized the affections as much as Clovelly and Grasmere. Wilson, who was coming from the Warwickshire direction, on his great cycling-tour, 'lay' at Woodstock partly because he was too tired to push on and do the remaining six (he says it was eight) miles, partly because he wanted to sleep 'at a quiet country inn.' From Woodstock to Oxford the road goes over a wide expanse of pleasant flat country between the rivers Glyme and Thames. It is country that King Charles I and his Cavaliers rode over many times in the Civil War. Wilson made the journey gently throughout the forenoon and reached Oxford about lunch-time. An afternoon stroll gave him the glance at Oxford that was sufficient to take his heart at once by storm. He wrote: 'I have seen as much that made me feel alien as that made me feel at home since I came to England, and have been made on the whole to love America more rather than less... but Oxford! Well, I am afraid that if there were a place for me here, America would see me

[1] R. S. Baker, II, 95.

again only to sell the house and fetch you and the children — and yet I have not seen a prettier dwelling
than ours in England.' This was on Wilson's first
visit, in 1896. On his second visit, in 1899, he writes:
'I have, of course, gone about Oxford, this time looking
about me with the keenest and most constant interest;
turning into quads; penetrating beyond quads to delightful secluded gardens.' His biographer believes that
the Oxford quadrangles, in part at any rate, were responsible for his vision, realised in time, of a recon-
structed Princeton.[1] Oxford, he said, was more beautiful and more fascinating than Cambridge; and yet,
when actually present in Cambridge, he began to wonder, as even Oxford men themselves do, whether anything *could* be more beautiful. Wilson became lyrical,
describing the 'Backs,' and the College bridges thrown
over the Cam, the noble buildings of Trinity, King's,
and St. John's, the spacious, serene lawns, 'the beauty
and peace and sweet air of the place.'

The English journeys were a real holiday for Wilson;
they proved (and they also widened) the sympathy of a
man who was sometimes thought to be deficient in this
quality. He was sympathetic to English scenes and
they to him. He found the people congenial. In spite,
however, of his bantering talk about selling the American house, he had not the slightest desire to settle in
England, and he had no friends there. He was an
American professor, with an especial interest in politics.

The college professor and the college president are,
by reason of their natural aptitude and of their special

[1] R. S. Baker, II, 80.

training, the class most sensitive to the characteristic features of the traditional English life. James Russell Lowell, Professor of Literature at Harvard since 1855, appointed Minister to the Court of St. James's in 1880, had an interesting and useful career as a diplomatist there, but he remained essentially the man of letters and the Harvard professor. He had been in England before, first in 1852, when he had visited Oxford, Cambridge, and some of the Cathedral cities; and in 1876 when Oxford gave him the degree of D.C.L. When he came again in 1880 he wrote to Mr. Norton: 'I like London and have learned to see as I never saw before the advantages of a great capital. It is, I think, a great drawback for us that we have as many as we have in the States.' London is a good capital, having a good slice of the countryside within itself. 'I have only to walk a hundred yards from my door,' wrote Lowell, 'to be in Hyde Park where, and in Kensington Gardens, I can tread on green turf and hear thrushes sing all winter.' He retained his critical faculty, however, and could mock at some things in England with charming piquancy.[1]

College professors tend to be critical, in addition to being sensitive to the romantic and æsthetic attractions of England. Sometimes their artistic sense and their critical faculty find difficulty in reconciling themselves to the same thing. One of Harvard's greatest presidents, a worthy representative of austere Puritanism, fought in his soul against the seductiveness of the Anglican Cathedral, and then succumbed. This was

[1] See Ferris Greenslet, *J. R. Lowell* (1905), 196, 199.

Charles W. Eliot, while still a young college teacher, on his first visit to Europe. He had recently married and was travelling with his wife. He writes to his mother:

> As you will see by Ellen's letter, we are giving special attention just now to English cathedrals, and very beautiful they are. I can quite understand what a hold the buildings and the services have on all educated Englishmen. I am a republican and a Unitarian and a Utilitarian, and yet I like amazingly to hear the church service in these vast and beautiful monuments of Catholicism. I am quite looking forward to our next Sunday in Durham where we can go to the Cathedral twice in one day. And yet, in a practical point of view, the heaping up of these services with their canons, deans, choristers and vergers is a monstrous cost, and for very little profit on any Protestant theory, for the Cathedral towns are now mostly small and the attendance on the service almost nothing. At Salisbury and Ely my family was the largest part of the audience.[1]

Evidently Eliot was a little troubled in mind about choosing between his Utilitarianism and his romantic spirit. He could not, like Fenimore Cooper about thirty years earlier at Cambridge, go quite so far as to say, he heard 'our own beautiful service in our own beautiful tongue' — a familiar and comforting experience after the deep-mouthed chants of the canons of French Cathedrals. Yet Eliot was clearly sensitive to a similar experience as Fenimore Cooper's.

The Americans in England have left many remarks about the English character. One of them, a philosophic college professor who resided in England, mainly in Oxford, during the World War, and who on a fine day

[1] H. James, *Charles W. Eliot* (1930), I, 156. This visit took place in 1865.

could be seen meditating on a seat by the bank of the Cherwell, wrote a whole essay on this subject. The world thinks that the Englishman is dominated by convention. He is not.

What governs the Englishman is his inner atmosphere, the weather in his soul. It is nothing particularly spiritual or mysterious. When he has taken his exercise and is drinking his tea or his beer and lighting his pipe; when in his garden or by his fire, he sprawls in an aggressively comfortable chair; when, well-washed and well-brushed, he resolutely turns in church to the east, and recites the creed (with genuflexions if he likes genuflexions) without in the least implying that he believes one word of it; when he hears or sings the most crudely sentimental and thinnest of popular songs, unmoved but not disgusted; when he makes up his mind who is his best friend or his favourite poet; when he adopts a party or a sweetheart; when he is hunting or shooting or boating, or striding through the fields; when he is choosing his clothes or his profession — never is it a precise reason or purpose, or outer fact that determines him; it is always the atmosphere of his inner man.

This 'weather in the soul' is not defined; but whatever it may be, 'it is also a witness to some settled disposition, some ripening inclination for this or that, deeply rooted in the soul. It gives a sense of direction in life which is virtually a code of ethics, and a religion behind religion.... It is a mass of dumb instincts and intelligences, the love of a certain quality of life, to be maintained manfully.' Inarticulate, tied to hopelessly stupid little dogmas and platitudes, from which the clever visitor turns away in despair, the Englishman still retains a personality of attractiveness. He prefers the country to the town. He may be shy and a little lonely, yet outwardly he is most hospitable, and the best of comrades for the time being. He is not by nature a missionary or a conqueror, for he has no settled design; he has only the instinct of exploration. 'He carries his English weather in his heart wherever he goes, and it becomes a cool spot in the desert, and a steady and sane oracle amongst the deliriums of mankind. Never since the heroic days of Greece has the world had such a sweet, just, boyish master. It will be a bad day for the human race when scientific blackguards, conspirators, churls and fanatics manage to supplant him.'[1]

This sympathetic stranger had discovered a beautifully healthy England, hidden from most foreigners: the England of the countryside, and of the poets, domestic, sporting, gallant, boyish, of a sure and delicate heart. Yet he had never the slightest tendency or desire himself to become an Englishman. 'Nationality and religion are like our love and loyalty towards women: things too radically intertwined with our moral essence to be changed honourably, and too accidental to the free mind to be worth changing. The free man is a citizen of the world who can appreciate another country and enjoy life in it, without in the least being tempted to abandon his own.'

In a summer after the war an American man of letters stopped off at Salisbury to see the Cathedral and its serene and gracious close.

'Star-scattered on the grass,' and beneath the noble trees, lay New Zealand soldiers, solitary or in little groups.

[1] G. Santayana, *Soliloquies in England* (1922), No. 9.

Later, at the Inn, I was shown to a small table, where sat already a young Englishman in evening dress, at his dinner. As I sat down opposite him I bowed, and he returned it. Presently we were talking. When I said that I was stopping expressly to see the Cathedral, and how like a trance it was to find a scene so thoroughly English full of New Zealanders lying all about, he looked puzzled. It was at this, or immediately after this, that I explained to him my nationality.

'I shouldn't have known it,' he remarked.

I pressed him for his reason, which he gave somewhat reluctantly, I think, but with excellent good will. Of course it was the same old mother-tongue.

'You mean,' I said, 'that I have not happened to say *I guess*, and that I don't, perhaps, talk through my nose? But we don't all do that. We do all sorts of things.'

He stuck to it. 'You talk like us.'[1]

Evidently the Englishman and the American found that they had much in common. In 1833 Oliver Wendell Holmes, on his first visit to England, passed himself off at Portsmouth, apparently with ease, as an Englishman, in order that he might be shown over the Naval dockyard.[2]

The abiding motive which urges men and women to leave their country for a time and to travel in foreign parts is not simply the call of the beautiful or of the strange. It is something deeper, the *Wanderlust* of the Aryans, of the people who made the first momentous migrations out of which the world grew. Americans and English seek each other's country with a persistence

[1] Owen Wister, *A Straight Deal* (1920), 221–22.

[2] Morse, *Life and Letters of O. W. Holmes* (1896), I, 84.

which surmounts every obstacle, social, political, economical; and they have always done so, since the first ship reached the other side. The motive has *Wanderlust* in it, but it is more than that: it is the homing instinct too. There is in the soul of the American and the Englishman alike that vague atavistic attraction, that odd recollection of a common social heritage, which expresses itself in the haunting feeling, on arrival, that he 'has been there before.' This was the sensation of Fenimore Cooper when he first landed at Liverpool, and of Captain Marryat when he first landed at New York; and of countless others, vocal or silent. Away from home they are at home; a new sky but a familiar spirit meets them.

Coelum non animum mutant qui trans mare currunt.
They change their *sky* but not their *mind*, who cross the sea.

THE END

INDEX

William III, 17

Williams, Roger, 13–15

Willis, Nathaniel P., 99, 121, 122; his *Pencillings*, 121

Willoughby, Francis, 10, 11

Wilson, John (Christopher North), 99

Wilson, Woodrow, 211, 255, 257, 260–69

Winslow, Edward, 8–10

Winthrop, John, 8, 11; his *History of New England* quoted, 8–11

Winthrop, John, Jr., 16

Wister, Owen, 273, 274; *A Straight Deal*, 274 n.

Woods, C. A., 263

Woods, Kathleen P., *The True Story of Captain John Smith*, 5 n.

Woolman, John, 37–41; his *Journal*, 19, 37–41

Worcestershire, Henry James in, 220–22

Wordsworth, William, Emerson's visit to, 126, 127, 129, 130; Woodrow Wilson and, 264, 265

World War, the, England in, 257

Wye, the river, 265

Yale College, 146

Yorkshire, Irving in, 110, 113, 114